P9-DJA-181

THE SPIRIT OF COMPROMISE

THE SPIRIT OF COMPROMISE

Why Governing Demands It and Campaigning Undermines It

AMY GUTMANN

AND

DENNIS THOMPSON

PRINCETON UNIVERSITY PRESS

PRINCETON AND OXFORD

Copyright © 2012 by Princeton University Press
Published by Princeton University Press,
41 William Street, Princeton, New Jersey 08540
In the United Kingdom: Princeton University Press,
6 Oxford Street, Woodstock, Oxfordshire OX20 1TW

press.princeton.edu

All Rights Reserved

Library of Congress Cataloging-in-Publication Data

Gutmann, Amy.
The spirit of compromise : why governing demands it
and campaigning undermines it / Amy Gutmann and
Dennis Thompson.
p. cm.
Includes bibliographical references and index.
ISBN 978-0-691-15391-9 (hardcover : alk. paper)
1. Political planning—United States. 2. Decision making—
United States. 3. Compromise (Ethics) —United States.
4. Consensus (Social sciences) —United States.
5. Democracy—United States. I. Thompson, Dennis F.
(Dennis Frank), 1940– II. Title.
JK468.P64G87 2012
320.60973—dc23
2011053123

British Library Cataloging-in-Publication Data is available

This book has been composed in Melior

Printed on acid-free paper. ∞

Printed in the United States of America

1 3 5 7 9 10 8 6 4 2

For Michael Doyle and Carol Thompson

Contents

INTRODUCTION

Compromise is difficult, but governing a democracy without compromise is impossible. Anyone who doubts either the difficulty or the necessity of compromise need only recall the heated politics of the summer of 2011 in Washington, D.C., when a sharply divided Congress confronted the need to raise the sovereign debt limit of the United States. Compromise appeared to be the only way to avoid further inflaming the financial crisis and risking an unprecedented governmental default on the debt. With the approach of the August 3 deadline (after which the government would no longer be able to pay all its bills), many observers doubted that any compromise could be reached in time.

The spirit of compromise was in short supply. Only at the last moment—on the evening of July 31—was President Barack Obama able to announce that leaders in both the House and the Senate had reached an agreement. Congress and the White House would now compromise. Yet criticism of the compromise abounded on all sides. The best that supporters could say for it was that its terms were less bad than the consequences of doing nothing. The episode stands as a dramatic reminder that compromise is the hardest way to govern, except all the others.

Why is compromise so hard in a democracy when it is undoubtedly necessary? Much of the resistance to compromise lies in another necessary part of the democratic process: campaigning for political office. Though valuable in its place, campaigning is increasingly intruding into governing, where it is less helpful. The means of winning an office are subverting the ends of governing once in office. It is only a slight exaggeration to say that in the United States "every day is election day in the permanent campaign."[1] The effects of a continuous campaign—along with the distorting influence of media and money that it brings—encourage a mindset among politicians that makes compromise more difficult. Systematic rejection of compromise is a problem for any democracy because it biases the political process in favor of the status quo and stands in the way of desirable change.

Privileging the status quo does not mean that nothing changes. It just means that politicians let other forces control the change. The status quo includes not only a current state of affairs but also the state that results from political inaction. In the deeply divided politics of 2011, rejecting congressional compromise on raising the debt ceiling would not have left the economy unchanged. A status quo bias in politics can result in stasis, but it can also produce unintended and undesirable change.

The resistance to democratic compromise is an-
chored in what we call an uncompromising mindset,
a cluster of attitudes and arguments that encourage
standing on principle and mistrusting opponents. This
mindset is conducive to campaigning but inimical to
governing. Resistance to democratic compromise can
be kept in check by a contrary cluster of attitudes and
arguments—a compromising mindset—which favors
adapting one's principles and respecting one's opponents. It is the mindset more appropriate for governing
because it enables politicians more readily to recognize
opportunities for desirable compromise. When enough
politicians adopt it, enough of the time, the spirit of
compromise prevails.

Politicians have complained about the decline of the
spirit of compromise, but they have not seen fit to restrain the clamor of campaigning. Political scientists
have exposed the harmful consequences of misplaced
campaigning, but they have not connected this problem with these mindsets and their implications for
democratic compromise.[2] Understanding the mindsets
can help show how the tension between campaigning
and governing creates difficulties for compromise, and
how a better balance between campaigning and governing supports possibilities for compromise.

The influence of campaigning is not necessarily
greater than other factors that interfere with compromise. Compromises are difficult for many reasons,
including increased political polarization and the

escalating influence of money in democratic politics. But the uncompromising mindset associated with campaigning deserves greater attention than it has received. First, it reinforces all the other factors. Even sharp ideological differences would present less of an obstacle to compromise in the absence of the continual pressures of campaigning that the uncompromising mindset supports. Second, for compromise to play its proper role in the process, politicians and citizens need to understand not only the partisan positions and political interests that influence compromise but also the attitudes and arguments that resist or support it. Third, unlike some of the other factors, such as ideological polarization, campaigning is an essential and desirable part of the democratic process. It becomes a problem only when it interferes with governing—another equally essential part of the process.[3]

In an era characterized by the permanent campaign, the balance in democratic governing needs to shift more toward the compromising mindset and the promotion of political compromises that it makes possible. Our defense of compromise in democratic governance is consistent with—indeed requires—a vigorous and often contentious politics in which citizens press strongly held principles and mobilize in support of boldly proclaimed causes. Social movements, political demonstrations, and activist organizations are among the significant sites of this kind of politics. The citizens who participate in these activities play important roles in democratic politics. But their efforts would be in vain if the democratic process of governance did not produce public benefits that citizens seek, and protect rights that they cherish. The success of democratic politics ultimately depends on how our elected leaders govern—and therefore inevitably on their attitudes toward compromise.

Two Compromises

To begin to diagnose resistance to democratic compromise, consider two pieces of historic legislation—the Tax Reform Act of 1986[4] and the Patient Protection and Affordable Care Act of 2010.[5]

The Tax Reform Act was the most comprehensive tax-reform legislation in modern American history, achieved only after years of failed attempts.[6] The historic effort began without much fanfare. In his State of the Union address in 1984, President Ronald Reagan called merely for a study of the problem, with a report to be submitted after the election. Congressional Democrats did not think he was serious about reform. Walter Mondale, his challenger in the election, showed no interest in making tax reform an issue. Mondale was not eager to say more about it after the less-than-enthusiastic reaction to his comment about taxes in his acceptance speech at the Democratic National Convention: "Mr. Reagan will raise taxes, and so will I. He won't tell you. I just did."[7]

The hard work on the bill began quietly, with experts meeting secretly in the Treasury Department. The proposals that came out of Treasury were turned into a bipartisan compromise, forged with the support of President Reagan, Democratic House Ways and Means Committee Chairman Dan Rostenkowski, and later with the help of Republican Chairman of the Senate Finance Committee Bob Packwood and Democratic Senator Bill Bradley.

All the supporters of the Tax Reform Act gained something they wanted, but they all also made concessions that flew in the face of their most principled reasons for supporting comprehensive tax reform in the first place. Democrats were glad to end loopholes for special interests and the wealthy, but they also had to agree to lower the top tax rate more than their strong commitment to progressive taxation would support (from 50 percent to 28 percent). Republicans won the lower marginal tax rates, but they also had to accept the elimination of some $30 billion annually in tax deductions, which would result in the wealthy contributing a higher percentage of income tax revenues than they had in the past.

Compromises—even the most successful ones, like the Tax Reform Act—never satisfy pure principles. After the act was passed, its supporters rallied to its defense, hailing it as landmark legislation. It was—if compared to previous or subsequent tax reform. But judged by the moral principles invoked even by its staunchest supporters—whether principles of progressive taxation and or those of the free market—the Tax Reform Act fell far short. A respected scholar of tax law compared the Tax Reform Act to a series of principled tax reform plans and found it lacking: "We are advised that this is the most sweeping legislation in fifty years, that it is a model of fairness and equity...I am not at all convinced by the propaganda."[8]

Now fast-forward to the efforts to pass a health-care reform bill in 2009–10.[9] Health care was an important issue in the campaigns leading up to both the Democratic primary and to the general election in 2008. Most of the presidential candidates set forth proposals that were more detailed than is usual in a campaign. Barack Obama came late to this debate, offering his health-care plan after other candidates had presented theirs.[10] But once in office, Obama made reform a priority. At first, he signaled that he was open to compromise on the details of his proposal and left the negotiations largely to congressional leaders. Relying on congressional leaders was essentially the same strategy that President Reagan had followed with tax reform. But the political landscape had changed since then. Throughout the 1990s, Republicans had begun more often to unite in the manner of a parliamentary minority, a strategy that drastically reduced the possibilities for bipartisanship.

When Congress was unable to reach bipartisan agreement on health-care reform by the August 2009 recess, the campaign in effect began again, with opponents taking advantage of the break to mobilize opinion against the pending proposals—often distorting them in the process. The upshot was to end whatever small hope there might have been for bipartisan compromise. Reformers then turned to the task of compromise within the Democratic Party, a challenge that turned out to be almost as formidable.

The first bill passed with only a five-vote majority in the House in November 2009. The Senate passed its own bill on the day before Christmas. As the leaders in the House and Senate were trying to hammer out a compromise between the two significantly different bills early in 2010, a special election in Massachusetts erased the Senate Democrats' filibuster-proof majority and caused many moderate Democrats in both the Senate and the House to reconsider their support. The campaign mentality returned with a vengeance. The reform proposals had to be divided into separate bills, a rarely used legislative procedure (reconciliation) invoked to gain final passage, and the ultimate measures rendered less comprehensive than any of the original proposals.

Although the Affordable Care Act was not bipartisan, the process that produced it was just as much a compromise as was the Tax Reform Act. All those who voted for health-care reform gave up something that they thought valuable, and they agreed to disagree about greater cost controls, the nature of the mandate for universal coverage, insurance coverage for abortion services, abortion funding, and the inclusion (or exclusion) of a public option (a government-run insurance agency that would compete with other companies). Although all who supported this compromise evidently believed the legislation would be better than the status quo, they also believed that the compromise bill could have been still better if only their opponents had been less obstinate.

These two historic efforts vividly underscore how difficult it is to achieve compromise on comprehensive reform on major issues in the U.S. political system. Although nearly everyone agreed that tax reform was long overdue and health care in dire need of change, political leaders struggled to reach these agreements, and the agreements fell far short of what reformers had sought. For the health-care reform bill to pass, it took an epic push by a president enjoying a majority in both houses and willing to stake the success of his first year in office on passing the bill. And the majority supporting this compromise was—with the exception of one lone vote among 220—exclusively within one party. Both efforts addressed major problems that had proved resistant to reform for many years, but only the Tax Reform Act was widely considered to be a significant improvement over the status quo. Many critics of the Affordable Care Act thought it was worse than doing nothing, and many supporters thought that it was better only than doing nothing.

Not even a crisis can ease the way of compromise. Although the consequence of failing to reach a compromise to raise the debt ceiling in 2011 was high risk of governmental default and a further financial crisis, the process of reaching the compromise was also agonizingly difficult, and the agreement—unlike the tax and health-care reforms—provided only a short-term fix. Achieving compromise on any of the many complex issues on the democratic agenda is always a challenge, not only with those initiatives that deal with taxation, health care, and the debt but also with job creation, education, immigration, and the many other matters about which citizens and their representatives deeply disagree.

Characteristics of Compromise

Before further exploring how the mindsets revealed in these episodes help or hinder compromise, we need to clarify the nature of compromise that is typically at stake in democratic politics.

In general, compromise is an agreement in which all sides sacrifice something in order to improve on the status quo from their perspective, and in which the sacrifices are at least partly determined by the other sides' will.[11] The sacrifice involves not merely getting less than you want, but also, thanks to your opponents, getting less than you think you deserve. The sacrifice typically involves trimming your principles.[12] We call these defining characteristics of compromise *mutual sacrifice* and *willful opposition*.

Although many kinds of compromise share these characteristics, legislative compromises—agreements that produce laws—do not always function in the same way as the kinds that are more commonly discussed, such as compromises to avert a war or create a peace in international politics or compromises to conclude deals in commercial transactions. Unlike major international compromises, legislative bargains are not negotiated with an ultimate threat of force in the background (though sometimes legislators speak of nuclear options and act as if electoral death is the end of the world). Unlike common commercial deals, the bargains struck by legislators are not primarily financial. Legislative compromises usually implicate principles as well as material interests.

The character of legislative compromise is shaped by its distinctive democratic and institutional context. It takes place in an ongoing institution in which the members have responsibilities to constituents and their political parties, maintain continuing relationships with one another, and deal concurrently with a wide range of issues that have multiple parts and long-range effects. The dynamics of negotiation in these circumstances differ from the patterns found in the two-agent, one-time interactions that are more common in most discussions of compromise.

Although some of the conclusions we reach concerning legislative compromise have implications for negotiation in other circumstances, especially in other lawmaking institutions, we concentrate specifically on legislative compromise in the United States, especially the Congress. Conclusions about compromise—even more so than many other concepts in political theory and practice—depend heavily on context. To make progress in understanding legislative compromise, we need to focus on how it operates and the specific challenges it confronts in American democracy in our time. The U.S. Congress is a critical case in part because its performance in recent years has been so widely condemned as dysfunctional. If we can find greater scope for compromise in this hard case, we might reasonably hope to find it in other political institutions.

Within the arena of legislative compromises, we need to distinguish between what may be called classic compromises and other consensual agreements. Classic compromises express an underlying and continuing conflict of values: the disagreements among the parties are embodied in the compromise itself. Other consensual compromises are based on an underlying convergence of values or what is often called "common ground." These agreements set aside the original disagreement and conclude in a complete consensus.[13]

Consensus on common ground is a lofty goal, and politicians never tire of claiming that they are seeking it. During the Republican primary in 2011, former Massachusetts Governor Mitt Romney declared: "Leaders [are successful] not by attacking their opposition but by finding common ground where principles are shared."[14]

Some advocates of consensus see it as a way to promote the value of community. Still others believe that it is more likely to produce the best laws and policies. All in effect urge politicians to base legislation on common ground shared not only between ideologically opposed parties but also among most citizens who do not have highly developed political ideologies. All citizens want a better life for themselves and their children; all want security, decent health care, a good education, and the like. The hope seems to be that a consensus would form on this common ground.

Few doubt that consensus is desirable if it can be found, and most agree that it is usually preferable to the standard form of compromise, which leaves all parties dissatisfied. But the common ground is more barren, and the possibilities for basing legislation on it more limited, than the inspiring rhetoric in its favor might suggest. Yes, a consensus existed among legislators and citizens that the tax system needed to be revised and that the health-care system needed to be reformed. Everyone agreed that the tax system should be made fairer and that health care should be made affordable for more people. But this general consensus on the need for reform did not translate into a common-ground agreement on the particular provisions of either a tax or a health-care reform bill. To produce reform legislation, specific terms had to be negotiated, and as is usual at this level, the common ground became fractured terrain.

In the context of a polarized politics, an additional problem with counting on common-ground agreements is that trying to find the usually small points of convergence in the middle is likely to prove less effective than combining big ideas from the partisans. Describing how they managed to gather a majority on their politically diverse commission on fiscal responsibility, co-chairs Alan Simpson and Erskine Bowles emphasize the value of "shared sacrifice" that comes from "bold and big" compromises. "The more comprehensive we made [our proposal], the easier our job became. The tougher our proposal, the more people came aboard. Commission members were willing to take on their sacred cows and fight special interests—but only if they saw others doing the same and if what they were voting for solved the country's problems."[15]

Classic compromises are sometimes also distinguished from what are called "integrative agreements," also known as "problem-solving," "value-creating," or "win-win" solutions.[16] Long the favorite of many writers on negotiation, they offer the prospect of an agreement in which both sides gain over the status quo, and neither side sacrifices. (The lack of sacrifice is why it does not count as a classic compromise.) The much-cited example, devised by Mary Parker Follett, the pioneering scholar in this field, features two sisters who both want the same orange.[17] The classic compromise solution is simply to split the orange. But it turns out that one sister wants only the juice and would throw out the peel. The other sister wants only the peel for a cake, and would discard the pulp. If they recognize that they have different interests in the orange, they could reach an integrative solution: one would take all of the pulp, the other all of the peel. Both would gain, and neither would sacrifice anything. The tactics that negotiation experts propose for reaching integrative agreements include expanding the pie, logrolling, creating symbolic compensation, and discovering new options.

Like the consensus agreements they resemble, the opportunities for achieving integrative agreements are scarcer in legislative politics than some of their enthusiasts imply.[18] Most of the examples of successful integrative agreements involve individuals or groups trying to resolve specific financial disputes rather than the kind usually faced in the ongoing negotiations that take place in legislatures. When legislators seek integrative solutions, they often use tactics of logrolling or expanding the pie. Logrolling typically requires the government to spend more money in order to satisfy the legislators' favored causes. Special interests then prevail over the public interest. By expanding the budgetary pie, older generations typically load more debt onto younger or future generations.

Health-care reform shared a feature of this problem. It expanded the budgetary pie by universalizing health insurance, but it fell short of coming to clear and certain terms with the rapidly rising costs of health care. For many supporters as well as critics of the reform, expanding the budgetary pie without fully facing up to escalating health-care costs is part of the ongoing problem, as these costs rapidly continue to rise. Only a classic compromise, which would include measures that more fully control costs and entail some sacrifice on all sides, could begin to deal with this problem.

While integrative approaches can be productive, legislative opportunities to achieve win-win solutions that serve the public without any sacrifice are rarely available. Legislators are much more likely to find themselves confronting conflicts that cannot be resolved without sacrifice on all sides. If they want to make gains over the status quo, they will have to give up something of value. They will not have the luxury of hoping for the pure win-win solutions that some negotiation theorists promise. They will just have to compromise.

Fortunately, the mindset and practices that encourage classic compromise are often the same as those that offer the best chance of finding common ground and integrative agreements. We can cheer on politicians when they search for common ground, but we should not let their failure to find it cast doubt on the value of the less exalted classic compromise.

Mindsets of Compromise

The compromising mindset displays what we call principled prudence (adapting one's principles) and mutual respect (valuing one's opponents). In contrast, the un-compromising mindset manifests principled tenacity (standing on principle) and mutual mistrust (suspect-ing opponents). Return now to the Tax Reform Act and Affordable Care Act, and notice how the defining char-acteristics of compromise—mutual sacrifice and will-ful opposition—map onto these mindsets.

To accomplish tax and health-care reform, both sides had to give up something of value. The need for mutual sacrifice makes compromises inherently difficult. Citi-zens and their representatives have different interests and values, and they naturally resist giving up some-thing they care about, especially if they believe that one of their core principles is at stake. Supporters of the Tax Reform Act and Affordable Care Act believed that the compromises would improve the status quo, but at first they clung tenaciously to their principles. The compro-mise came about only because the principled positions that reformers espoused—a simple and transparent tax code or universal health-care coverage, for example—did not survive intact in the tangled process that pro-duced the final legislation.

To achieve these compromises, the mistrust so easily generated by willful opposition also had to be partially suspended. Enough of the legislators respected their opponents enough to make the necessary concessions. But in both cases, the uncompromising mindset that fosters mistrust of one's opponents hung over the pro-cess and its aftermath. Supporters as well as opponents of both reforms continued to believe that the legislation could have been better if the other side had been less inflexible. Even in the case of the Tax Reform Act, resistance was relentless, and discontent rife. The opponents, under the influence of the uncompromising mindset, nearly prevailed. The supporters, only fitfully taking up the compromising mindset, nearly yielded.

Health-care reform fared worse. Both the process and the outcome were more widely and severely criticized than any aspect of tax reform. The suspicion and mistrust characteristic of the uncompromising mindset lingered among Democrats themselves. The progressive wing faulted their leaders and the president for betraying campaign promises. Moderate Democrats complained that their colleagues did not appreciate how public opinion had shifted against the reform, and how vulnerable they would now be in the 2010 midterm elections.

Political polarization is no doubt an important part of the story of why compromise is so difficult. It exacerbated the willful opposition that beset both tax reform and health-care reform. The lower degree of party polarization in the 1980s may also partly explain why bipartisan compromise was possible in the case of the Tax Reform Act but not the Affordable Care Act. But partisan polarization does not shed much light on why compromise on health-care reform within the Democratic Party was at least as difficult as compromise on tax reform between the two parties. Nor is it sufficient to account for the widespread assumption that compromise on health-care reform could have been more successful if Senators Orrin Hatch and Ted Kennedy had been able to collaborate as they had many times in the past.[19] Polarized profiles do not necessarily prevent political opponents from reaching agreement. Even when the ideological positions of political opponents are polarized, compromising mindsets can make a difference.

Political scientists disagree about the source of polarization in the United States. Is it only elites who have become more polarized, or also the electorate, and, if both, to what extent are elites the cause?[20] Identifying more precisely the source of polarization could help in targeting reforms to reduce the obstacles to compromise. (We consider a range of reforms in chapter 5.) But the value of our analysis does not depend on resolving the disagreement about whether the public, elites, or both are the ongoing source of polarization. Whatever the source, a compromising mindset can go a long way toward mitigating the negative effects of polarization on the dispositions toward compromise of both political leaders and voters, and an uncompromising mindset can exacerbate those effects. The characteristics of these mindsets and their connection to campaigning and governing apply to both political leaders and voters.

Some observers are so impressed by the influence of polarization that they give up any hope of compromise and see partisan domination as the only alternative.

They begin by describing increased polarization among not only political elites but also engaged partisans, who spend most of their lives with like-minded peers. The uncompromising views of these engaged partisans, coupled with the "disappearing center" in American politics, create strong incentives against compromise: "any serious attempts at compromise by party leaders would almost certainly produce a backlash among their most politically active and informed supporters."[21] These doubters of compromise conclude that "successful efforts at bipartisan cooperation and compromise are unlikely. That leaves partisan dominance as the only viable means of overcoming gridlock in Washington."[22]

Strong partisans may still chase the tantalizing dream that the next election will settle the matter, once and for all. My party will gain control and push through its agenda, undiluted. Yet in contemporary American politics it is unlikely that one party will regularly gain complete control at the national level (securing the presidency, the House, and the reliable sixty votes needed to overcome a filibuster in the Senate). And if one party were to gain control, it would still face the daunting task of making compromises within its own ranks. Neither can we look for a single, strong leader to come to the rescue—the president, as some have urged. No president can prevail as long as Congress remains recalcitrant.

There is no escape from compromise. Politicians are likely to continue to work in a strongly divided partisan environment, and they need to find ways to reach agreements if they expect to govern well. Looking more carefully at differences between the Tax Reform Act and the Affordable Care Act can help clarify what makes compromise more or less possible in polarized partisan contexts.

Among the many differences between the processes that led to these compromises on tax reform and health-care reform, one stands out as the most relevant to understanding the mindsets that prevailed. Tax reform was not an issue in the campaigns before or after the compromise. Health-care reform was an issue in the 2008 and 2010 elections, and no doubt will be an issue in campaigns to come. Partly as a result, the process that led to the Tax Reform Act was more responsive to the compromising mindset, and the process that produced the Affordable Care Act was more susceptible to the uncompromising mindset. The uncompromising mindset inherent in campaigns gained less traction during the tax reform negotiations and therefore had less influence in the legislative process later. Furthermore, the permanent campaign that reinforces that mindset has been more conspicuous in recent years than it was in the mid-1980s when the Tax Reform Act was negotiated.

Campaigning in an uncompromising style—making unconditional promises and discrediting rivals—plays a moral as well as a practical role in democratic politics. It enables candidates to communicate where they passionately stand on important issues and to differentiate themselves from their opponents. It is a necessary element of an electoral system with competitive elections and is therefore a legitimate part of the democratic process. But so is governing. To govern, elected leaders who want to get anything done have to adopt a compromising mindset. Rather than standing tenaciously on principle, they have to make concessions. Rather than mistrusting and trying to defeat their opponents at every turn, they have to respect their opponents enough to collaborate on legislation.

Here is the internal tension in political compromise: the democratic process requires politicians both to resist compromise and to embrace it. The uncompromising mindset that characterizes campaigning cannot and should not be eliminated from democratic politics. But when it comes to dominate governing, it obstructs the search for desirable compromises. The uncompromising mindset is like an invasive species that spreads beyond its natural habitat as it roams from the campaign to the government.

The democratic process itself in this way gives rise to the problem of compromise. Some theorists have emphasized that the democratic process requires compromise, and some have also found constraints on compromise in the process itself.[23] Others have argued that negative attitudes toward compromise are "rooted in the nature of political life."[24] We go further and show that the democratic process itself creates obstacles to compromise by means of the tension between the mindsets manifested in governing and campaigning. We examine how the domination of campaigning over governing feeds the uncompromising mindset, making legislative compromise even more difficult than it needs to be.

We do not try to provide a causal explanation for the Tax Reform Act, Affordable Care Act, or other compromises. The causes are multiple, and the outcomes usually overdetermined. We focus here on the role of the mindsets in the process of political compromise. Appreciating the attitudes and arguments that make up the mindsets—and their connection to campaigning and governing—is an essential step in any effort to address the problem of compromise in democracy.

Many observers blame Republicans for the uncompromising spirit that pervades current American politics, pointing out that they have become more extreme and intransigent in recent years. But it would be a mistake to dwell on who is most to blame at the moment. The uncompromising pressures are persistent in a democratic process in which campaigning dominates governing. If it so happens that one party is more responsible for the polarization at a particular time, this should not distract us from the broader problem that needs to be addressed to make room for responsible governing.

The problem of compromise in American democracy has always been challenging. It becomes harder still with the rise of the permanent campaign. The relentless pressures of campaigning—which call for an uncompromising mindset—are overtaking the demands of governing—which depend on a compromising mindset. Because legislating in the public interest is all but impossible without compromise, the domination of campaigning over governing has become a critical problem for American democracy, and increasingly for other democracies. By recognizing the pressures of the permanent campaign and the dynamics of the mindsets in play in democratic politics, politicians, the media, and, above all, the voting public would be more likely to find ways to address this problem.

In the pages that follow, we first show why compromise matters—its value and its limits (chapter 1). Next we analyze the uncompromising mindset (chapter 2) and the compromising mindset (chapter 3), and in each case explore their links to campaigning and governing. Then (in chapter 4), we explain how the democratic process—with its dual demands of campaigning and governing—depends on both kinds of mindsets. Finally (in chapter 5), we consider some reforms that could create a better balance between campaigning and governing, as well as the mindsets that typify them. That balance is essential to making more space for desirable compromises in the democratic process. When the spirit of compromise fades, the spirit of the laws suffers.

1

⬥

VALUING COMPROMISE

Do citizens value compromise? Americans are ambivalent about it. That is the most striking pattern revealed in surveys of public opinion in recent years. The ambivalence shows itself in public attitudes toward politicians who compromise and also toward compromise itself. In a typical survey, the vast majority of Americans said they prefer leaders willing to compromise, but at the same time two-thirds of all the respondents also said that they "like politicians who stick to their positions, even if unpopular."[1]

When asked about compromise in general, most Americans like the idea. In numerous surveys over the past several decades, large majorities of Americans declared themselves in favor of political compromise in general. Even after the sweeping Democratic victory in the midterm elections in 2006, three-quarters of the public continued to call for compromise.[2] Although Democrats then controlled both houses of Congress and more states than before, nearly 60 percent of

Democratic voters still wanted their leaders to compromise with Republicans in Congress (though not necessarily with President Bush).

There are limits to this enthusiasm for the idea of
compromise, however. After the strong Republican
comeback in the 2010 congressional midterm elections,
a majority of Americans—a large majority of Republicans and a minority of Democrats—said that they prefer
political leaders who stick to their positions without
compromising.[3] The favorable attitude toward the idea
of compromise erodes when the political landscape
shifts this dramatically.[4]

Nor does the favorable attitude normally transfer to
support for particular compromises. Public support for
compromise in general is greater than support for compromise on any particular issue, whether it be immigration, taxation, government spending, the environment,
the war in Iraq, or especially abortion. On most issues,
"openness to compromise is inversely linked to the importance people place on the issue."[5] Most Americans
like compromise the most on the issues they care about
the least.

There are limits here too. Opposition to particular
compromises is likely to fade in face of a crisis, at least
for the moment. When compromise is a condition of
avoiding an imminent disaster that could harm nearly
everyone, the vast majority of the public—Democrats
and Republicans included—support a compromise.[6]
Faced with the risk of government default on its debt,

even a majority of Tea Party supporters said that they would support a compromise that included tax increases as well as spending cuts.[7] But once the immediate threat is averted, the critics of the compromise come out in full force. Especially when a compromise in a crisis is reached through an acrimonious process, no one is pleased with its terms. The debt ceiling agreement in August 2011 gave everyone plenty to criticize on principled grounds, and criticize it they did.[8]

Compromise is necessary and desirable in a democracy—most Americans usually agree. But particular compromises are contestable—most Americans usually want to contest them. Within the limits just described, a popular posture in democratic politics seems to be: say yes to compromise, but no to compromises. The ambivalence toward political compromise is not peculiar to the Americans who respond to surveys. It reflects the inevitable tension between seeing the need to compromise to make political progress and sensing the loss of something valuable in making a compromise.

When generally opining about democracy, writers enthusiastically praise compromise. For some, like Thomas Vernor Smith, an early-twentieth-century politician turned theorist, it is what makes politics "an ethical enterprise."[9] But when faced with making concessions on particular issues they care about, most stand their ground. Smith drew the line at Chamberlain's appeasement at Munich. Smith went on to propose a curious division of labor that would institutionalize the tension between compromises and the value of compromise. Conscientious citizens can resist making particular compromises while accepting the general need to compromise if they allow "moral middlemen"— politicians—to "do the dirty work" for them.[10]

Political philosophers have long recognized the same tension and shown the same ambivalence, though not always in the same direction. Edmund Burke, the eighteenth-century conservative thinker and British statesman, declared that "all government, indeed every human benefit and enjoyment, every virtue, and every prudent act, is founded on compromise and barter."[11] But as a politician, he famously refused to compromise with his constituents when their will went against his judgment.[12] The nineteenth-century liberal theorist John Stuart Mill was known as an uncompromising radical to his contemporaries. But when elected to Parliament, he was quite willing to make deals and support concessions to achieve relatively modest gains.[13]

It might seem that conservatives favor compromise in principle but not in practice, whereas liberals declare themselves against compromise in principle but then readily compromise in practice. But consider the Pew Center's interpretation of its 2007 survey on attitudes toward compromise: "Democrats tend to favor compromise in principle, but not in practice, while Republicans favor compromise in practice, but not in principle."[14] This is precisely the reverse of the Burke/Mill contrast. The more plausible interpretation of these comparisons is that the attitude toward compromise is not inherent in either ideology or party. Both liberals and conservatives can favor compromise in principle while resisting it in practice—and vice versa. So can Democrats and Republicans. In the modern welfare state, even partisans who want less government have to legislate to get it, and that often means they have to compromise. Attitudes toward compromise depend much more on the relative power of the parties at any particular time, the specific issues in question, and the mindsets of the individuals making the judgments.

What is clear, however, is the persistent disconnection between the attitudes toward compromise in general and the inclinations to make particular compromises. Nothing is more common in political negotiation than praise for the idea of compromise coupled with resistance to realize it—unless it is criticism of the idea followed by an acceptance of a particular compromise.

This resistance stands in the way of appreciating the value of compromise in the practice of democratic politics. Politicians and citizens tend to discount the general value of compromise when they come to make decisions about particular compromises. To give compromise its due, we therefore need to relate its general value to decisions about particular compromises. Appealing, as some theorists do, to the general need for stability or the preservation of civil peace is not enough.[15] We need to put the general value of compromise back into decisions about particular compromises. Once we have understood the general value of compromise in this way, we can better understand the attitudes and arguments—the mindsets—that support and impede compromising in practice.

Costs of Not Compromising

If compromise is becoming more difficult, why should we be concerned? After all, some compromises are undesirable, and politicians should sometimes stand resolutely on their principles and oppose legislation that violates those principles. The chief reason to be concerned is that the greater the resistance to compromise, the greater the bias in favor of the status quo.

The status quo offers no assurance even of stability, let alone of progress by anyone's standards. The first value of compromise in practice is simply that it enables improvements in the existing and ongoing state of affairs. Democratic politics, which represents conflicting points of view, cannot produce change without some mutual accommodation. Almost no major change can happen without major compromises. Without compromise on health care and taxation or other major issues, the status quo prevails, even if it preserves a policy that serves everyone's interests poorly and even if it leads to a major crisis.

The key question to ask of any compromise is: does the proposal (or any feasible alternative) represent an improvement over the status quo? This question in effect brings the general value of compromise to bear on the decision about particular compromise. Although compromises are typically seen as, and often are, the products of unprincipled bargaining and reinforcements of the prevailing balance of power, they are also the primary—and often the only—means by which democratic politics can improve on the status quo.[16]

The status quo can of course sometimes be defended against any of the available alternatives. Some political scientists have observed that legislative inertia induced by resistance to compromise may not be a problem when voters do not want Congress to act—for example, during the period of large budget surpluses in the late 1990s. But they also recognize that it becomes a serious problem when voters "believe the government should take some action to alleviate a problem."[17] In a changing world where serious problems get worse when left unaddressed, few would argue for legislative inertia as a general policy.

There can of course be reasonable disagreement about whether a particular compromise actually is an improvement over the current state of affairs. Opponents of a health-care compromise might agree that it would be better than the current system but believe that accepting it will prevent an even better reform in the future. Or they may think that accepting it now will lead to bigger government, which they count as a worse outcome on balance than what they regard as only a modest improvement in the health-care system. These and other considerations may be good reasons for one or the other side to oppose a particular compromise, but they do not support a general resistance to compromise. They do not create the presumption against compromise that animates the uncompromising mindset, which tends to dominate in contemporary American politics.

A general resistance to compromise implausibly presumes that the status quo is always more defensible than a compromise, or that it is always a mistake to yield something to one's political adversaries even when they are willing to yield something to you. Privileging the status quo in this way is not consistent with either a principled liberal or a principled conservative stance toward politics. Liberals do not always favor the change that compromise can bring, and conservatives do not always oppose it. The same holds for moderates, libertarians, socialists, and other advocates of principled political ideologies. It depends on whether the change advances their principles compared with what the status quo will advance, absent new legislation.

A strong psychological resistance to compromise flows from the fact that the costs of not compromising are never equal for everyone in democratic politics. The costs depend on the difference between what credibly can be achieved by compromise and what the status quo offers without compromise. This difference will vary according to what matters most to the compromising parties and those they represent. Because political compromises rarely "split the difference" between what all parties hope to achieve, resistance may flow from people's fear that in compromising they will lose more or gain less than their opponents, whom they already are disposed to distrust. Even when all parties stand to gain a great deal, such anticipatory resentment of unequal gain (or loss) prompts an overly generalized opposition to compromise.

This generalized opposition to compromise feeds on the same zealous factionalism that, as Madison famously observed in Federalist No. 10, "divide[s] mankind into parties, inflame[s] them with mutual animosity, and render[s] them much more disposed to vex and oppress each other than to co-operate for their common good."[18] On the one hand, people who resist all compromise out of generalized fear and distrust of their opponents may become their own worst enemies, which Madison also warned against. On the other hand, when people refrain from thinking they will lose too much or gain too little, they can begin to consider the costs of not compromising. Exposing the source of such generalized fear and seeing how to avoid it can be an important step forward.

Another source of general opposition to compromise is the perpetual hope that there is more to be gained (or less lost) in the future by not compromising now. Opponents of compromise who take this approach in effect recognize that they have to defend their resistance to compromise by showing that the proposed change is not really an improvement over the status quo. But notice: they are not opposing compromise as such. They are bringing additional, indirect consequences into the calculation of whether a compromise is better than the status quo—longer-term effects on the policy in question and other related policies. Once they adopt this perspective, they open the door to the proponents of the compromise to introduce their own broader considerations. These include the effects on the possibility of future cooperation as well as other consequences for the democratic process.

Those considerations point to the second important value of compromise that is often lost when compromises are thwarted. Resistance to compromise undermines practices of mutual respect that are essential for a robust democratic process. Mutual respect expresses a constructive attitude toward, and willingness to engage in good faith with, one's political opponents. It is based on a principle of reciprocity, which is at the core of many different conceptions of democracy.[19] Reciprocity seeks mutually acceptable ways not only of resolving disagreements but also of living with the disagreements that inevitably remain.

Mutual respect is consistent with a wide range of nonviolent means of reaching agreement, which include bargaining, provided it is in good faith. But mutual respect excludes means—including some other kinds of bargaining—that are intended to degrade, humiliate, or otherwise demean opponents who themselves demonstrate a willingness to negotiate in good faith (or would demonstrate it were they not being disrespected). Regularly resisting compromise in these ways not only harms the citizens who stand to benefit from a particular compromise but also diminishes the prospects for other compromises in the future. When parties enter into negotiations in bad faith, deliberately misrepresent their opponents' positions, and refuse to cooperate even on matters on which they could find agreement, they undermine the relationships of respect that are necessary to sustain any morally justifiable democracy under the modern conditions of deep and persistent disagreement.

Vulnerabilities of Compromise

Recognizing these two values of compromise—enabling mutually beneficial improvements and promoting mutually respectful politics—may still not be sufficient to tip the balance in favor of a particular compromise. Taking into account another consideration, arising from characteristics inherent in all compromises, is necessary to appreciate fully the case for encouraging them. Political compromises need to be encouraged because, even if people recognize the costs of not compromising, they will find that all compromises by their nature are perpetually vulnerable to criticisms from all sides.

The philosopher George Santayana captured the dual nature of the aversion felt toward compromise: It is "odious to passionate natures because it seems a *surrender*, and to intellectual natures because it seems a *confusion.*"[20] The sense of surrender comes from the fact that every compromise sacrifices something of value to each side and gives rise to suspicions that, but for the base motives of the other side, the agreement could have been better. The sense of confusion comes from the fact that compromises are combinations of principles that are often contradictory. A brief discussion of each of these reactions can bring out how they obscure the value of compromise.

First, the surrender. Attitudes toward a compromise are path-dependent. How a compromise is reached affects how it is evaluated. This is due to one of the distinctive features of compromise already mentioned: a compromise manifests an opposition of wills. It is this opposition of wills that fuels the anticipatory resentment that your party will gain less, or lose more, than your opponents. If you overcome this generalized resistance and agree to a compromise, a key question in deciding whether your party got a fair deal in a compromise is whether the other party bargained in good faith. Given the inevitable uncertainty about motives in legislative negotiations (and the near certainty that the motives are at least partly political), the circumstances are singularly ripe for distrust. Often even minor procedural manipulations (such as the reconciliation tactic used by the Democrats in passing the health-care bill) can be taken as signs of bad faith and give rise to suspicions that the process has been unfair. You may be willing to give up a principle if the process is fair, but if it is not, you understandably see an already-bad bargain as even worse. The compromising adds insult to injury. Because the process of political negotiation is always imperfect, it is easy to fasten on the immediate insult and forget the prospective benefit of the agreement.

Second, consider the confusion also almost impossible to avoid. A compromise is not meant to be coherent or principled in the way that laws are ideally supposed to be. Even if we aim at coherence in law, it is a mistake to think that we can generally achieve it in compromise. The aim in compromise is to give something to all parties, which means that the result almost always will be internally contradictory. The outcome will not be satisfying if judged from the perspective of any single principle or set of principles—whether yours or those of your opponents. You will reject nearly every possible compromise if you try to anticipate the outcome by testing it against a coherent theory of justice. By its nature, a compromise will almost never satisfy such a theory. It is not simply that the compromise will fall short, as does most legislation, but that it will include elements that are jointly incoherent and inconsistent with any single theory.[21]

Politicians engaged in negotiations often claim that they are seeking common ground. If they are successful in finding common ground, the agreement would rest on shared principles or interests. It could then be coherent, and it might even represent a consensus. In 2008, both parties in Congress agreed on a package of housing legislation intended in part to help thousands of financially troubled borrowers hold on to their homes.[22] Assume that many legislators supported it at least in part to help the homeowners, some supporting it primarily to stabilize the turbulent housing market and some merely to protect the lenders. This agreement would then constitute a rare consensus: it can be coherent as long as the varying reasons underlying it do not yield an internally conflicting policy. Another recent example of bipartisan convergence began to develop in 2011 on ending some farm subsidies, long thought to be invulnerable. Many conservatives now criticize them as intrusions into the free market; many liberals oppose them for promoting environmentally harmful overfarming; and both regard them as a form of corporate welfare.[23]

These kinds of common ground agreements are morally as well as politically attractive because they have a principled coherence, judged from all sides. They resemble what philosophers call an overlapping consensus. Citizens with fundamentally different moral views—like conservatives and liberals approaching farm subsidies—may agree on relevant principles but for different reasons, which are drawn from their own potentially conflicting moral perspectives.[24]

Analogously, legislators set aside conflicting parts of their perspectives in order to reach a shared agreement. What is sacrificed is agreement on their principles, but no concession is made in the content of the agreement. For this reason, their consensus may not even be a compromise, strictly speaking. Furthermore, these successes in achieving an overlapping consensus are often due less to a search for common ground or a change of attitude than to a change in the political circumstances. The convergence on ending some farm subsidies, for example, took place because one side began to care more about reducing the deficit, the other about decreasing environmental damage, and both found that they could resist the influence of the big agribusinesses.

Consensual agreements are not impossible, but they are rare and, in polarized politics, only getting rarer. Because the possibilities for achieving common ground are limited, exhortations in praise of it add to the vulnerability of classic compromises, which by comparison look like confused surrenders. Yet it is the classic compromises that offer the best hope. This is because the major issues in legislative debates usually represent deep divisions on fundamental questions about the role of government, the nature of justice, and the liberties, rights, and responsibilities of citizens. The broad issues on which many Americans generally favor legislative compromise—taxation, government spending, health care, cost controls, job creation—are unlikely to be addressed at all if legislators hold out for common ground. Where the need for compromise and the compromising mindset are greatest, the prospect of finding common ground is likely to be poorest.

So if compromise is to be achieved on major issues of the day, we should expect to value agreements that are less coherent and less appealing than those that rest on common ground or overlapping consensus. The Tax Reform Act of 1986 combined measures (eliminating loopholes that favor the wealthy) that reflected liberal principles but others (lowering the marginal rates on top incomes) that violated those principles. The same measure also created a conflict with conservative principles, but in reverse. The tensions in the Affordable Care Act of 2010 showed themselves less in whether a national health-care system ideally should cover all citizens than in whether it should also reduce health-care costs (and by how much), allow all those satisfied with their plans to keep them, and induce more or fewer providers to participate. The proponents argued that some of the provisions in the act (for example, pilot programs to promote best practices or the competitive exchanges) would eventually reduce total costs, but it was generally recognized that a significant tension between increased coverage and escalating costs—and therefore a principled problem of nationwide affordability— would persist for many years.

In the compromise that produced welfare reform in President Clinton's second term, the confusion is embedded in the very title of the legislation—"The

Personal Responsibility and Work Opportunity Reconciliation Act of 1996."[25] Work opportunity suggests a choice: here is a job—take it or leave it. But the act itself did not (and probably could not) provide enough jobs for those who wanted them, while the work requirement was intended to take away any practical or moral choice. Personal responsibility meant that everyone who wanted welfare must have a job or be registered to accept one. More critically, some children—who cannot credibly be held personally responsible or be said to have an opportunity to choose—would lose their support if their parents had no job. The compromise legislation was controversial at the time, with several of Clinton's senior advisers resigning in protest when he signed the bill. Yet later most observers agreed that the reform, for all its flaws and internal incoherence—a classic legislative compromise—significantly improved on the previously existing system.[26]

Limits of Compromise

Compromise in democratic politics is not sufficiently appreciated, but it should not be grandly elevated to the prime virtue of the democratic process. Compromise has its limits. They apply to its domain, process, and content.

Although the uncompromising mindset should not dominate governing, it is well suited to its *domain* of

campaigning. But campaigning is far from the only domain in which uncompromising mindsets play a major
role in democratic politics. Uncompromising politics
also has a large and valuable place—often far more productive than in electoral campaigns—in social movements, political protests, demonstrations, and activist
organizations, and in their surrogates in government.

Without the uncompromising, compromise would
need no defense. With the uncompromising at their
flanks, compromisers gain bargaining power. As commentators have noted, liberals need radicals.[27] Burkean
conservatives need right-wing conservatives, and moderates may need them all. As political theorists and political scientists have long recognized, contestation is
at least as important as consensus in a democracy.[28] Far
from being a necessary evil, contentious politics is an
essential part of the democratic process, and an inevitable context for compromise.

Among the most uncompromising activists in recent
American political life have been the supporters of the
Tea Party, a populist movement that began in 2009 and
rapidly grew in numbers and influence.[29] Promoting
various conservative and libertarian causes, including smaller government, lower taxes, and reduced debt
and budget deficits, the movement was credited with
electing dozens of new legislators in many states and
as members of Congress.

Tea Party supporters expressed more opposition
to compromise during the early stages of the budget

controversies of 2010–11 than did other Republicans, who opposed compromise in greater proportions than did Democrats. A national poll conducted in April 2011 found that only 28 percent of Tea Party supporters wanted the Republican leadership to compromise on the budget even if refusal to compromise meant a government shutdown. Sixty-eight percent favored a no compromise position. Among all Republicans, 56 percent said their leaders should stick to their positions while 38 percent favored compromise.[30] Speaking on the Senate floor about the budget in April 2011, Rand Paul, a first-term senator elected with Tea Party support, expressed the movement's dominant attitude toward compromise in general: "They say that compromise is the ideal. They tell the Tea Party, you need to compromise. But you know what the compromise is? They want to raise your taxes."[31]

The Tea Party movement gave voice to views that were held by a substantial minority of citizens. It succeeded not only in electing many new legislators but also in shifting the national Republican agenda to the right on many issues. Republican leaders in Congress found themselves brokering difficult compromises within their own party, and they also found their hand strengthened in negotiations with Democrats as a result of the intransigence of their Tea Party Caucus. Democrats objected to the policies and principles of the movement, but they could not easily dismiss the uncompromising tactics. Many of their own supporters

criticized the Democratic leadership for being too accommodating and pressed their leaders to use the same
tactics. Both sides recognized that political forces that
adamantly reject compromise can aid in changing the
legislative agenda.

The evolution of the Tea Party movement also reminds us that this kind of rejection also has limits.
The limits became apparent as the representatives
sent to Congress faced a dilemma—a choice between
legislating or protesting. On the one hand, if legislators, including those who represent uncompromising
movements, are to be effective in governing, they have
to compromise. Some newly elected legislators with
Tea Party sympathies wanted to be effective and made
early compromises that alienated much of their grassroots base. Only six months after his election, Massachusetts Senator Scott Brown incurred the wrath of
his Tea Party supporters by deciding to vote in favor
of financial reform. In July 2010, the Greater Boston
Tea Party declared itself "greatly disappointed" by
Brown's decision and warned that he would suffer the
consequences.[32]

On the other hand, the alternative—which some political scientists believe is more likely in the case of the
Tea Party—is to continue in the same uncompromising
mode. "The loose construction of Tea Party activism is
more likely to produce political theater among competing agitators than to foster reasoned compromise within
the GOP or between Republicans and Democrats in

Washington." This approach may help "keep base supporters attentive and angry," but it is not conducive to
bringing about legislative change or to expanding the
movement itself.[33] This "just say no to compromise"
approach also showed signs of frustrating even most
Tea Party supporters. Over just three months' time in
2011, as Tea Party supporters shifted from two-thirds
majority opposition to two-thirds majority support for
congressional compromise on raising the debt limit,
many criticized intransigent Republican as well as
Democratic legislators.[34]

Even in the domain of political movements, citizens
who want their representatives not only to change
the nation's political agenda but also to pass better
legislation often recognize the limits of saying no to
compromise. This recognition of the need to compromise among supporters of political movements means
that legislators who are adamantly uncompromising
risk alienating those who are seeking positive legislative change. "I thought they were playing with my
future," said a Tea Party supporter in Texas who was
among the majority favoring compromise. "You have
to come to some kind of resolution. It can't just be 'kill
everything.'"[35]

As public recognition of the need for legislative
compromise increases, including among supporters
of political movements, so too does the incentive to
compromise increase for politicians caught up in the
permanent campaign. While some legislators swept

into office by a political movement will not compromise even if it means losing the next election, others will more readily compromise when they perceive that the political winds have shifted and compromising will help them win the next election. This means that the extent to which the voting public signals its appreciation of the need for legislative compromise is likely to make a significant difference in legislators' willingness to compromise, once they are in office. The limits of compromise in the domain of grassroots political movements therefore do not translate directly into limits on legislative compromise.

The *process* of compromising provides the basis of the second limit on compromise. If a compromise is arrived at in a process that does not show at least minimal mutual respect—for example, if it comes about as a result of improper threats, deception, or manipulation employed by one or both parties—people may reasonably not only criticize but also reject the deal, even if it creates a better policy than the status quo. A process of compromise that involves undue pressure may encourage further polarization over time, weaken a democracy's capacity for cooperation, and make future compromises more difficult. Under any of these improper procedural conditions, a compromise is less likely to be fully accepted.

"Improper" points to a difficulty in deciding whether the compromise should be rejected, however. Because threats, deception, and manipulation cannot be completely ruled out in politics, the kind and degree of pressure at work in the process is relevant to deciding what limits to place on compromise. Threats to shut down the government may be unwise or even irresponsible, but they do not by themselves invalidate a compromise reached in a process in which they played a role. The threats refer to a relevant and possible outcome of the failure to reach agreement. In contrast, the threats of violence against some members of Congress, as occurred in the health-care controversies, could have no such justification.[36] If that kind of pressure—a violent threat—had been decisive in an ongoing, otherwise peaceful democratic process, the compromises that resulted would not have been legitimate.

Who participates in the process also matters. When a compromise significantly affects people who are not represented in the negotiations, we should look more skeptically at its terms. The parties making the deal may correctly believe that it is an improvement over the status quo—for them and their constituents. Whether it is an improvement for those who are not or cannot be represented in the negotiations is another matter. Deals that set immigration policy or create long-term environmental risks warrant special scrutiny because some of those who are most affected are least represented. Because immigrants—prospective, legal, and illegal—have little voice, we should raise serious questions about compromises (and failures to compromise) that legislators make in this area of policy. Similar and even more challenging questions should be raised about legislation that imposes high risks on future generations who cannot be directly represented, and whose very existence depends on which policies are adopted by present generations.[37]

Are there some compromises that simply because of their *content* should not be made? No doubt. To acknowledge this limit, we do not need to turn to the history of iniquitous deals with dictators that is often invoked to paint compromise in the colors of appeasement. We do not have to try to distinguish between compromising with Hitler and Stalin.[38] We can find more pertinent cases closer to everyday politics.

Recall the special deals that Senate Majority Leader Reid evidently offered to secure the votes on the health-care reform bill in December 2009. Arguably, some of these could be defended as the product of customary logrolling, minor concessions necessary to win support for the larger compromise. But at least one—the so-called Cornhusker Kickback—went too far by just about everyone's lights. To secure the sixtieth vote he needed to break the filibuster on the health-care reform bill, Reid included $100 million in extra Medicaid funding just for Nebraska, hoping to win the support of the state's wavering Senator Ben Nelson.[39] During merger negotiations with the Senate, House leaders effectively made the argument that the "kickback" was a preferential deal—a slice of pork that was not available to other states and was given only to attract Nelson's support. The deal was so blatantly discriminatory that even Nelson himself finally spurned the special treatment, and the funding disappeared in the final bill. When the beneficiary of a compromise thinks it unfair, that is a fairly good sign that the concessions have gone too far.

While we cannot count on seeing such a reliable sign too often, we may be able to find other indications that compromise has gone too far—aspects of the content of an agreement that should raise doubts. In chapter 3, drawing on John Stuart Mill's conception of compromise, we suggest several factors to be considered in deciding whether to accept a compromise. Whatever the basis of such decisions, the judgment is bound to be complex and variable, depending on the particular compromise and the particular circumstances. That may not be the case with all kinds of compromises, but it is surely so with legislative ones. The number of issues, the multiple parts of each, their long-term effects, the representational roles of the negotiators, and their continuing relationships in an ongoing institution make the calculation more complicated than the two-agent, one-time interactions common in other settings. Political compromise has limits, but they can be captured only in a context-sensitive judgment, not in a general formula claiming to serve for all seasons.

What does this complexity imply for appreciating the value of compromise? First, it is a mistake to try to find unconditional principles that separate acceptable from unacceptable compromises. In chapter 2, we show why attempts to set absolute limits on compromise do not succeed and how they reinforce the uncompromising mindset and thwart agreements that most people would reasonably regard as improvements.

Second, it is also a mistake to try to decide in advance whether your principles (even if not absolute) should prevent you from accepting a final compromise. Your principles may be constant when expressed in general terms (protect individual liberties, provide equal opportunities, and so on). But how you would apply the principles, and how you would weigh them against one another, can and often does change as the details and implications of the legislative proposals are clarified and as new alternatives that no one had previously imagined are introduced.

Representative Dan Rostenkowski (reflecting the views of most liberal Democrats) entered the later stages of the negotiations on the Tax Reform Act in conference committee firmly opposed on principle to the Senate's proposal to lower the top rates to 27 percent.[40] But this reform had not only won a majority in the Senate, it also had captured the public imagination. Then, as the negotiations progressed, he "came to understand" that a top rate of 27 percent could be just as progressive as his own plan—provided that the loopholes that benefited the wealthy were eliminated. Furthermore, he saw that "if he accepted the Senate's rates as the starting point ... [t]he senators would come under tremendous pressure to accept his [the House's] corporate reforms." In the end, the final bill (which by then included a top rate of 28 percent and a reduction in the hidden surtax) combined reforms from both bills, a compromise that served the general interest and (perhaps not incidentally) left no extra revenue for further compromises that would serve only special interests.[41]

When abortion funding became an issue in the health-care reform debate, Bob Casey, a pro-life Democratic senator from Pennsylvania, said he could not support any bill that allowed the government to pay for abortions. He voted against the bill in committee. But when it became clear that his vote would be needed for final passage, he began to look for a compromise. Instead of the Stupak amendment in the House version of the bill (which many saw as a broader prohibition on government funding of abortion than current law already imposed), Casey reluctantly accepted the looser restrictions in the Senate bill (which required insurers, including the proposed government-run plan, to pay for abortions only with money from private premiums and to keep any federal subsidies in a separate account). But he insisted on adding an amendment that would increase services for pregnant women to help educate them on their choices. He argued that it "would empower many of those women to decide to keep their babies."[42] As he worked with other senators on the issue, he said he was "not drawing any lines in the sand...I just think that there's going to be enough momentum to get a bill passed that one issue—even one very important issue—will not prevent passage."[43] The shifting political circumstances enabled this senator, whose principles initially led him to oppose any compromise on abortion, to find a new approach—one not available in this form at the start of the negotiations. It went far enough to satisfy Casey and enough of his colleagues to win passage of the final bill.

Casey's late agreement to the health-care reform bill also illustrates a third important implication of the complexity of compromises. Even if you are inclined to compromise, you generally should not reveal your flexibility from the start. This is moral as well as strategic counsel. If you are seen as too eager a compromiser, you not only risk weakening your negotiating position but also can be criticized for failing to move the final compromise as far as possible in the direction of the principles to which you and your supporters are committed.

A fourth implication of their complexity is that particular compromises cannot be adequately evaluated as freestanding laws or policies. To appreciate the value of compromise, a decision to accept or reject a particular agreement must take into account a wider range of factors than those that would usually be considered in a judgment about the law or policy considered alone.

Certainly there is significant overlap in the grounds for judgment. For example, parties to a proposed compromise should try to decide whether it would bring about more social justice, individual well-being, or other improvements than would the status quo. If a health-care compromise brings about less social good than the status quo from the parties' perspectives, then they have a good reason, and usually a sufficient reason, to reject it.

So far, evaluating a compromise is not so different from assessing a freestanding law or policy. But judgments about a compromise also must consider whether any of the parties could have secured more by offering less (or holding out for more). Because compromise involves a contest of wills, compromisers have to make their best estimate about the motives of the other sides. Given the competitive nature of the negotiations and the diversity of influential parties who typically influence them, this estimate is bound to be fraught with uncertainty. The parties will be highly uncertain about their negotiating positions not only before but also after they reach an agreement. This reinforces the vulnerabilities—the senses of surrender and confusion—that we described earlier.

These vulnerabilities are likely to be reduced only by trying to promote a sense of mutual trust over time—for example, by means of long-term collegial relationships. One of the distinctive considerations in appreciating the value of compromise is therefore the question of the extent to which the compromise itself can further this kind of trust, or how the refusal to compromise can impede it.

Limits of History

We are likely to be disappointed if we look to history for conclusive lessons about the value of political compromise. Grand compromises such as those reached at the Constitutional Convention in 1787 are often cited as exemplars of moral courage, but just as often as testaments to moral cowardice. The judgments of history in these monumental cases are often as ambiguous as our judgments about compromises in our own time. They provide unequivocal support for neither a negative nor a positive view of compromise. What they can offer us is some additional perspective on both the moral vulnerabilities of compromise and the processes that can mitigate—but not transcend—those vulnerabilities.

Consider the two momentous compromises embodied in the original Constitution—the equal representation of states in Congress and the three-fifths representation of slaves.[44] The first combined proportional representation by population in the House (favored by the larger states) and equal representation in the Senate (favored by the smaller states). The second compromise—between the free and slave states—struck a deal between the view that only free citizens should count in apportioning members of the House and distributing taxes and the view that slaves should count just as fully, even though they could not vote. This compromise offended principles of equality, fairness, and respect for human dignity even more egregiously. Many people at the time thought so too. Of the two sets of compromises, the first is generally assumed to be less objectionable. If both were necessary to move in the direction of the greater good, then the unequal representation in the Senate seems to be the lesser evil.

But is it? One of the most eminent historians of the period, Jack Rakove, argues: "A case can be made that [the slavery compromise] turned out to have fewer costs than the other deal [unequal representation] the framers had to strike to complete their task."[45] It was not the three-fifths clause that gave the southern states the "leverage they needed to keep the Union safe for slavery, but rather the Senate, where the later Compromises of 1819–20 and 1850 did more to preserve the political equilibrium."[46] After Reconstruction and well into the twentieth century, their disproportionate representation in the Senate gave the southern states the political power to resist the movements for greater equality and civil rights for blacks. The defense of a compromise shifts depending on when it is judged, and even then these complex judgments remain contestable.

Not only are the relative merits of these compromises contestable; so is the question of their necessity. The chief argument offered for both is that they were required in order to secure the passage of the Constitution and prevent the dissolution of the union. The delegates to the Constitutional Convention knew that their handiwork would soon face the public in the process of statewide ratifications. It was not lack of skill or grit in bargaining that caused the northerners to concede on the slavery issue. They knew that a proposed Constitution that "struck a serious blow at slavery would never survive the hurdles of ratification."[47] The delegates therefore had their eyes on the ratification battle to come. In effect, they were already preparing for a campaign that required them, both individually and collectively, to defend the results of the convention. In this kind of campaign—unlike a zero-sum electoral contest that pits one candidate against another—all the delegates who support the proposal can win if they cooperate. Anticipating this kind of campaign (as distinct from conducting it) created enormous pressure on the convention delegates to compromise. (As we discuss in chapter 3, under special conditions, even electoral campaigning can facilitate compromising.)

Most historians agree that the unequal representation in the Senate was probably necessary to secure ratification, but even here there is disagreement about exactly why the concession was needed. The historical judgment of the slavery compromise is still more complex. Some of the major concessions the North made may not have been necessary at all.[48] South Carolina and Georgia, which needed federal help to cope with the increasing threats from Indians on their borders, might well have accepted a prohibition on importing new slaves, as long as they could keep the slaves they had. The fugitive slave clause might have been successfully opposed because the southern states believed that it would probably not be enforced effectively anyhow.[49]

The point is not to reach a conclusive verdict on whether this compromise was defensible but rather to suggest that assessments of major political compromises, even on the seemingly objective question of whether they were necessary and with all the advantages of hindsight, do not yield definitive yes or no judgments. After all these years of careful scholarship, uncertainty still surrounds the question of what was necessary and defensible.

Rather than taking any comfort in notable compromises of the past, we would do better to acknowledge the violations of basic moral principles involved even in those compromises that many defend (both then and now). These violations cannot be discounted even if it is true that the refusal to compromise would have left a status quo with even greater violations and would have made it more difficult to lessen injustice in the future. Because these historic compromises include extreme injustices as a core part of their moral incoherence, they make vivid how political compromise exemplifies the role of "dirty hands" in politics.[50] The strongest defense often still leaves a large residue of injustice, which is overridden but not erased by any good consequences that the compromises may have produced.[51]

No doubt there are compromises that should not have been made. An example sometimes cited is the Compromise of 1877, known as the "Corrupt Bargain," which effectively ended Reconstruction. (To win the support of the southern Democrats in the disputed presidential election of 1876, Republican Rutherford B. Hayes as president agreed to remove federal troops from the South.) Even when we find cases that should have been clearly opposed at the time, we are not warranted in concluding anything about the morality of compromise in general. Just as we should not use the widely accepted compromises of the past to reassure us about compromises we might make now, so we should not invoke the ignoble compromises of the past to move us to resist compromises we need to make now.

Nevertheless, historical examples can suggest some important lessons about the process of compromising— lessons that are largely independent of any overall moral assessment of the content of the compromises. Assume what almost all historians agree on: at least some (even if not all) parts of the constitutional compromises were necessary to improve upon the status quo and preserve the union. Set aside any more definitive judgments about the content of the particular compromises in order to ask: what conditions encouraged delegates to make these compromises?

First, and perhaps foremost, there were the "conciliatory habits of mind that most delegates to the convention possessed."[52] The delegates did not usually approach conflict simply by advancing their own interests but sought accommodations at critical junctures in the deliberations. Benjamin Franklin's role was more important than is generally assumed. As the "most persistent advocate of compromise," he intervened in the early weeks of the session when controversy about the basis of representation threatened to disrupt the convention. He encouraged the delegates to proceed "with great coolness & temper." He warned that "positiveness and warmth tend to create and augment discord and division in a great concern, wherein harmony and Union are extremely necessary to give weight to our Councils, and render them effectual in promoting & securing the common good."[53]

A second favorable condition: this temper of conciliation was easier to sustain because the proceedings were not open to the public. The convention adopted the rule "[t]hat nothing spoken in the house be printed, or otherwise published or communicated without leave."[54] The advantages of confidentiality in the convention have often been noted. Less often emphasized is that the secrecy could not have been justified, and the conclusions accepted as legitimate, had the proposed Constitution not been submitted to the people in the states for a final decision. Even when confidentiality is useful for securing compromise, it facilitates successful compromise only if coupled with an opportunity for public confirmation within a reasonable period of time.

A third condition that facilitated compromise consisted of small, sometimes even technical, procedural agreements that together probably made a significant difference. On the second day of the convention, the delegates adopted several rules that favored the spirit of compromise. One was a rule of mutual respect so obvious that we might think it gratuitous until we consider the practices of the contemporary Congresses. The rule simply required delegates to pay attention to one another: no reading, walking around, or conversing while a member was speaking. Another rule provided that any delegate could postpone the final decision on an issue until the following day, even if it had been "fully debated." Still another specified that a vote on any question should not prevent delegates "from revising the subject matter of it when they see cause."[55]

During the process of ratification a seemingly minor procedural concession—in effect a compromise about compromising—was key to success in several states.[56] Many representatives in the state conventions, not only the anti-Federalists, wanted to have a chance to offer amendments. They could cite reputable principles of popular sovereignty to make their case. But allowing amendments as a condition of ratification would have required another convention to resolve the conflicts among the various amendments that were likely to be proposed. The Federalists reasonably believed that the resulting chaos would doom ratification. They had therefore opposed allowing any amendments at all. But in the critical state conventions in Massachusetts and New York, they finally agreed to permit amendments—on the understanding that they would not be binding. The drafters of this compromise in New York were especially adroit: their three sets of amendments were called "explanatory, anticipatory, and recommendatory." Those who wanted to propose substantive amendments could not have been fully satisfied, but neither could they complain that their concerns had been completely ignored.

It is not true that political compromise gets no respect. Few people are as cynical as H. L. Mencken, who remarked, "A politician...has to make so many compromises...that he becomes indistinguishable from a streetwalker."[57] Most Americans say they want their legislators to compromise, and most politicians who try to govern effectively adopt a positive attitude toward compromise. Although some do not like to admit it, most tacitly accept something like the stance that Ronald Reagan took toward the "radical conservatives" in the California legislature who thought "'compromise' was a dirty word...[and] wouldn't face the fact that we couldn't get all of what we wanted today. They wanted all or nothing and they wanted it all at once...

I'd learned while negotiating union contracts that you seldom got everything you asked for."[58]

Compromise is essential for facilitating legislation to improve on the status quo and for cultivating the respect necessary for cooperation in democratic politics. Yet the political deck is stacked against compromise in many ways. The agreements produced by compromise, by virtue of their very nature, are vulnerable. They too easily become casualties of confusion, dispatched for their incoherence, if they have not already become victims of death by distrust.

We have suggested ways that the general value of compromise can be better appreciated, as politicians and the citizens who influence them confront the challenge of making particular compromises. To see how democracy could be made safe for compromise, we need to explore how the uncompromising and the compromising mindsets function. Specifically, we identify their strengths and weaknesses, and show why the uncompromising mindset fits with campaigning and the compromising mindset suits governing.

2

RESISTING COMPROMISE

Even when politicians may be willing to compromise, they are reluctant to admit it. Consider this excerpt from an interview with Representative John Boehner on CBS's *60 Minutes*, as he was about to become Speaker of the House after the Republican success in the 2010 congressional elections:

JOHN BOEHNER: We have to govern. That's what we were elected to do.

LESLIE STAHL: But governing means compromising.

BOEHNER: It means working together.

STAHL: It also means compromising.

...

BOEHNER: I made clear I am not going to compromise on my principles, nor am I going to compromise ... the will of the American people.

STAHL: And you're saying I want common ground, but I'm not going to compromise. I don't understand that. I really don't.

BOEHNER: When you say the word "compromise"... a lot of Americans look up and go, "Uh-oh, they're going to sell me out."

. . .

STAHL: ... you did compromise [to get all the Bush tax cuts made permanent]?

BOEHNER: ... we found common ground.

STAHL: Why won't you say—you're afraid of the word.

BOEHNER: I reject the word.[1]

Like many politicians, Boehner resists not just the word but also the mindset. He prefers to look for common ground, which seems to avoid having to admit that he has to give up anything. He can still stand firm on his principles and negotiate actively but guardedly with his opponents. The interview exemplifies the uncompromising mindset. The two characteristics of this mindset are principled tenacity, which rejects the sacrifice that compromise entails, and mutual mistrust, which inflates the willful opposition that compromise involves. Together they stand in the way of desirable compromises as well as undesirable ones.[2] Before analyzing each of these characteristics, we should explain how we understand the concept of mindset itself.

The Makeup of Mindsets

A mindset is a cluster of attitudes and arguments that incline an individual to organize thinking and action in a way that makes some considerations and choices more salient than others. It is a composite of cognitive and dispositional states—influencing both how one tends to conceptualize and argue about phenomena and how one is inclined to act on the conceptualizations and arguments. Mindsets are not always consciously adopted, but they can be consciously criticized, changed, and even abandoned—depending on the context—in favor of a different, competing mindset. Like the attitudes that social psychologists study, mindsets can be both "stable and situationally variable."[3]

Compromising and uncompromising mindsets are ways of thinking and acting that aid or impede the making of compromises. In politics they span ideological perspectives. Both liberals and conservatives can be influenced in their attitudes and actions by both mindsets. Moreover, the same individual politician can (and often does) adopt a compromising mindset at one time, and an uncompromising mindset at another. The mindsets are generally not embedded in the character of an individual. The political environment, including interactions with colleagues and incentives created by institutions, brings about shifts from one mindset to another.

Finding oneself in a campaign can trigger the uncompromising mindset. Being held responsible for passing legislation can activate the compromising mindset. Having a trusting collegial relationship with a colleague across the partisan divide can elicit the compromising mindset. Encountering disrespect by a colleague, whether in the other party or your own, can prompt an uncompromising one. How political institutions are structured—including the incentives and disincentives they create to spend time campaigning, fundraising, legislating, and even socializing with colleagues across the political spectrum—also influences the distribution of mindsets in the political process.

In political science, a close conceptual cousin to mindsets is framing, which has been described as "the process by which people develop a particular conceptualization of an issue or reorient their thinking about an issue."[4] Like mindsets, frames "give prominence to one consideration, or to a mix of considerations."[5] A mindset itself can be thought of as a kind of frame: as when a politician frames a negotiation as an occasion for standing on principle and defeating opponents. But frames also can influence a mindset: as when a politician frames the negotiation as part of a campaign, and is thereby primed to adopt an uncompromising mindset.[6]

The research on framing sheds some light on how mindsets function in politics. For example, media can create frames that influence the standards used by citizens to evaluate political leaders. If the media highlight stories about defense policy, citizens tend to base their evaluation of the president on their view of his performance on defense; if the stories emphasize energy issues, they will more likely judge him on his energy policy.[7] As we discuss in chapter 5, if the media frame the political process as a permanent campaign, this tends to reinforce the uncompromising mindset.

Other studies examine what happens when individuals are presented with more than one frame. How people react to these competing frames might help us to understand how politicians react to the competing mindsets, a common occurrence in politics. Although research on competitive frames is currently limited, it appears that competing frames do not simply neutralize one another.[8] The stronger ("more persuasive") frame can shift opinion in its direction even among those who continue to see a controversy through the alternative, weaker frame.[9] This suggests that the judgments encouraged by a frame—and encouraged by mindsets that function in similar ways—are open to challenge and subject to change. Furthermore, studies show that citizens can moderate the effects of elite-created frames if they engage in discussions with other citizens who hold varying opinions.[10] This may indicate that even those whose minds are primed by others can modify their mindsets.

Mindsets manifest a form of what psychologists call cognitive bias. But as we use the concept, the biases in mindsets do not necessarily lead to reasonable or unreasonable, moral or immoral conclusions. They do not produce either only positive or only negative influences on political thought and action.[11] But they do incline people to think and act in one rather than another direction.

An attitudinal and argumentative bias for or against compromise may be inevitable in politics. To process the enormous amount of information that politically engaged people need to make decisions and take actions, adopting the cues that the compromising and uncompromising mindsets provide may be necessary. But adopting only one of these mindsets, constantly over time, is not inevitable. Some of the same politicians who, while campaigning, stand tenaciously on principle and mistrust their opponents are able to shift to a compromising mindset while governing. Other politicians stick with the uncompromising mindset most but not all of the time they govern.

We do not view such mindset effects in the negative light that some social science research regards framing effects. Kept in balance, both the compromising and the uncompromising mindsets can serve a useful function in the democratic process, as we suggest later in discussing the productive tension between campaigning and governing. Nor do we treat mindsets primarily as a tool that elites use to manipulate public opinion. Mindsets shape the thought, attitudes, and actions of elites themselves. For understanding political compromise, the mindsets of leaders are at least as significant as the more-often-examined mindsets of citizens.

Most of the work on framing effects has focused on policy issues—how different frames tend to favor different conclusions on various public policies. In contrast, the mindsets of compromise structure thought, attitudes, and action about the process of politics more than about policy issues. They are about how to make laws rather than about what laws should be made. In this respect, the mindsets may be regarded as meta-frames.

Political theorists generally have not examined the content and function of mindsets in politics. They understandably may believe that mindsets lack the rigor and scope of a theory. But, as we show in this chapter and the next, the mindsets of compromise have a cognitive as well as an attitudinal structure. They presuppose moral values, express arguments, and imply theoretical commitments. Critical analysis of their structures could benefit from more normative attention by political theorists as well as from more empirical investigation by political scientists.

Principled Tenacity

"I will never compromise my principles." So says nearly every politician running for office or trying to stay in office. (If you doubt the ubiquity of this declaration, just try an Internet search with this phrase and its equivalents.) The declaration displays the first characteristic of the uncompromising mindset—principled tenacity.

Because compromises often require both sides to sacrifice some of their strongly held principles to enter into the agreement, compromises may be rejected because they are thought to violate a deeply held core value. Taking a stand against compromise itself comes to be seen as the only principled position: "It is not the principled partisan, however obnoxious he may seem to his opponents, who degrades our public debate, but the preening, self-styled statesman who elevates compromise to a first principle. For the true statesmen . . . are not defined by what they compromise, but by what they don't."[12]

Standing on principle is of course sometimes an admirable stance to take in politics. Edmund Burke's speech to his constituents in Bristol, in which he defended following his conscience against the opinion of his electors, still has resonance.[13] But how much of the resonance would remain had Burke stood tenaciously only on those principles that opinion polling told him that his electors would agree with and would therefore make them likely to reelect him? This would be quite contrary to the tenor of what Burke announced to his electors. He put them on warning that they should expect him to vote in Parliament against their opinions when his conscientious judgment required it, not when his political calculations advised it. Recall the core of Burke's speech: "Your Representative owes you, not his industry only, but his judgement; and he betrays, instead of serving you, if he sacrifices it to your opinion."[14]

Imagine a modern-day Burke standing before a crowd of his constituents and telling them that he will vote in favor of increasing their taxes or decreasing their entitlements whenever he conscientiously believes that they and their nation would be better served as a consequence. Profiles in courage like this still have the power to inspire, and they provide a source for the continuing influence of the uncompromising mindset. But the uncompromising mindset for which Burke spoke did not oppose compromising with other legislators when he thought the interests of his constituents or the nation demanded it. He also argued that "all government" and "every prudent act" is founded on compromise.[15] He embraced the general idea of compromise. Far from opposing all particular compromises, he publicly rejected only those that entailed merely deferring to his constituents' opinions.

Principled tenacity is easier if your vote is not decisive. Many of the cases in which legislators are praised for standing on principle turn out to be occasions on which they can oppose a compromise without bringing about its defeat. In legislatures, party leaders usually know in advance which members' votes they can afford to lose, and they can let members know when their support is not needed. The members can then vote their conscience or their constituents' preferences—without concern for the fate of the compromise, one way or the other.

In April 2011, more than one hundred Democrats and fifty Republicans in the House voted against the budget bill that avoided a shutdown of the federal government. They typically defended their votes as a matter of principle, probably sincerely so. Although some of these members would have voted against the bill no matter what, all must have known, by the time of the roll call, that the bill would pass without their support. In these circumstances, standing on principle may be perfectly acceptable, perhaps even praiseworthy. But we may take a less favorable view of principled tenacity in the very different circumstances in which the members' negative votes affect the outcome. The stand is scarcely praiseworthy when the votes block a compromise reasonably regarded as necessary to avoid consequences that would seriously harm the whole society.

If all politicians rejected all compromises that violate any of their principles, even when making improvements on the status quo required compromise, then no particular compromise would ever be acceptable. Yet some particular compromises surely should be accepted and others rejected. How can a politician consistently accept the general value of compromise but reject some particular compromises? There are two common answers. The first tries to distinguish compromises of principle from compromises of interest, rejecting the former while accepting the latter. The second answer accepts some compromises of principle, but not those that would violate a basic human value of some kind. Neither answer is satisfactory.

PRINCIPLES V. INTERESTS

"The genius of American politics," the philosopher Robert Paul Wolff once observed, "is its ability to treat even matters of principle as though they were conflicts of interest." He then added, parenthetically with a verbal wink, "It has been remarked that the genius of French politics is its ability to treat even conflicts of interest as matters of principle."[16] By treating principles as interests, compromise seems to become easier, whereas treating interests as principles seems make it harder. If we could distinguish disagreements about principles from those about interests, we could follow the common maxim: never compromise your principles, only your interests.

We would then distinguish material interests, understood as income, wealth, and the things that money can buy, from moral principles, understood as values to which individuals are committed as part of their identity or out of strong ethical conviction. When interests are at stake, it is thought to be easier to find a way for each side to give up something. When principles and related values are at issue, it seems that one or both sides are giving up more than anyone should. The difficulty of compromising would seem to diminish if we could transform disputes about principles into disputes

about interests. This approach—distinguishing principles from interests, and trying to transform the principles into interests—is often recommended by writers
on dispute resolution, because (it is assumed) interests
are amenable to bargaining, while principles are not.[17]

Many scholars as well as politicians have gravitated
toward this position, perhaps because it rests on a distinction that seems high-minded—between material
interests and principles of justice.[18] The "compromise-
interests-not-principles" maxim is frequently invoked
as the way to resolve the moral ambiguity in political
compromise. Michael Ignatieff, the former leader of
the Liberal Party in the Canadian Parliament and also
a well-known author of books on (among other topics)
political ethics, succinctly articulates this position:
"Sometimes sacrificing my judgment to theirs is the es-
sence of my job. Provided, of course, that I don't sacrifice my principles...Fixed principle matters. There are
some goods that cannot be traded."[19]

The maxim is appealing, and has become a rhetori-
cal staple of politicians on the campaign trail. One important reason for its appeal: strong principles matter,
whether in compromising or not compromising. They
serve as guideposts in judging whether a proposal is
pointing in the right direction—toward one's principles. But "never compromise your principles" suggests
that the principles are roadblocks, intended to stop a
political compromise dead in its tracks, rather than

guideposts, meant to draw attention to critical values at issue in the compromise.

"Never compromise your principles, only your interests"—neither its negative claim that principles cannot be compromised nor its positive claim that interests can be easily compromised is sustainable. The near-absolute ban on compromise based on moral principle turns out to reach almost all of democratic politics. Tenaciously standing on the principles of fairness and equity that were prominently invoked in the drive for tax reform in 1986 certainly would have blocked any compromise on tax reform. If universal health-care coverage is taken to be a principle that should not be compromised, there can be no policy that would cover less than the entire U.S. population (or the entire citizenry, if the principle is thought to apply only to citizens). Yet why would it not be both moral and practical, if no better alternative is available, to agree to cover more Americans than are presently covered, even if that involves compromising the principle of universal health-care coverage? Whatever the answer to this question, it cannot rest on the claim that universal coverage is a principle, not an interest.

The cost of health care to taxpayers is plausibly seen as an interest, but it would not be right in principle to agree to a compromise that escalated the cost of health care beyond what a healthy economy could sustain or what is needed to provide high-quality health care and better outcomes. The interest implicates a principle. The main problem is not that the distinction between interests and principles is fuzzy (it is), but rather that any such distinction—implying that interests may be compromised and principles should not—will disqualify too many potentially desirable compromises, most of which require some sacrifice of principle.

The operative idea behind the positive claim that compromising interests is acceptable seems to be that a material interest—especially when it can be put in monetary terms—is easy to trade off. Money is fungible; principles are not. An insurmountable problem with this claim is that few material interests in democratic politics, and almost no important ones, present themselves unattached to moral principles. Containing the cost of health care, for example, is connected to (among other principles) providing all individuals with the basic needs of life. To many people, satisfying basic needs is a core moral principle.

Most of the major material interests at issue in democratic politics—such as the fiscal health of Social Security, the extension of unemployment insurance, and the provision of foreign aid—are similarly inseparable from core principles of justice. Taxation obviously affects material interests, but one need only consider the claims made in debates about the estate tax or progressive taxation to see that the policies significantly implicate fundamental values. Advocates and opponents of different tax policies rest their cases in large measure on property rights and principles of distributive justice.

Another reason why "compromise your interests but not your principles" may be so appealing in politics is that interests seem to lend themselves to the simple technique of splitting the difference, whereas principles are thought to require all-or-nothing judgments.[20] This argument also is suspect. An acceptable compromise may or may not be one that splits the difference by finding an equal or midpoint division of interests. Whether the best available compromise splits the difference depends on the content and background conditions of the compromise, including the welfare, rights, respect, and other relationships among the parties. Splitting the difference does not escape the responsibility to assess the justice of the split.

Compromises of principle do not require all-or-nothing decisions any more than do compromises of interest. Principles can be—and most often are—realized only partially—more or less, not all-or-nothing. We implicitly accept this truth throughout our lives: with or without compromising, we are never likely to realize our most prized political principles (liberty, opportunity, justice for all) entirely or absolutely. Less lofty political principles, which are no less passionately held—such as a commitment to lower taxation and entitlement spending, or to provide universal health-care coverage and decrease its cost—even more clearly admit of gradations of realization. Compromises of principle and interest are in these critical ways neither morally nor practically distinct.

ACCEPTABLE V. UNACCEPTABLE COMPROMISES OF PRINCIPLE

The best recent attempt to distinguish acceptable from unacceptable compromises sets aside the distinction between principles and interests. The philosopher Avishai Margalit defends what he calls the "decent kind" of compromise. Most democratic compromises are "decent" and should not be rejected on the basis of absolute principles.[21] Proposed agreements should be compared to the status quo and then subjected to the morally messy processes of political negotiation. He would rule out few if any compromises that take place within the constraints of a constitutional democracy. The only compromises that are not decent are those that "perpetuate cruelty and humiliation," which he calls "rotten."[22]

Yet Margalit ends up advocating some violations of even his most basic principle. He supports compromises that permit cruelty and humiliation for an entire generation if the long-term benefits (in reducing cruelty and humiliation) are great enough. His absolute principle turns out not to be absolute after all. His attempt to draw a clear, principled line between the decent and the rotten fails for three reasons that frustrate the use of any such standard to determine in advance whether a compromise is acceptable.

First, any unconditional standard (at least, any politically relevant one) will block some decent compromises that improve on the status quo. This may be why Margalit refuses to rule out all compromises that perpetuate humiliation and cruelty. For the same reason, under some circumstances, rejecting compromises that perpetuate cruelty and humiliation for more than one generation could perpetuate even more cruelty and humiliation for even longer. The problem with driving a moral stake in the ground at one generation—or anywhere else—is that it arbitrarily limits the range of consequences that should be considered in assessing whether the compromise is decent, or a sufficient improvement over the status quo to count as decent even when it still perpetuates significant injustices, including cruelties and humiliations.

The second reason to be wary of any unconditional standard is the flip side of the first reason. Standing on an absolute standard to reject a compromise should not imply that any other compromise (which does not violate that standard) is acceptable. Surely we should reject some compromises that satisfy a minimalist standard of not perpetuating cruelty and humiliation for more than a generation.[23] Not even the maxim "compromise whenever the policy is an improvement on the status quo" is unconditional. Some compromises that improve on the status quo may block further progress that otherwise would be more likely—for example, by legitimating systematic deception and manipulation by relatively powerful and privileged parties. Even qualifications to the status quo maxim may be misleading when elevated into unconditional standards. We cannot unconditionally defend any preordained standard—whether substantive or procedural—or state all the conditions that constitute a sufficient defense. That is part of the distinctive nature of compromise.

A third reason to be wary of a predetermined standard follows from another characteristic of many compromises. No one can fully anticipate what the complex process of compromise can be expected to yield in most major legislative struggles. Achieving the best possible outcome will depend in no small measure on the nature of the negotiations and the evolving political context.[24] Before the fact, driving a principled stake in the ground and tenaciously refusing to move—if more than a negotiating tactic—is a prescription for thwarting progress that could be mutually beneficial. After the fact, a preordained standard is even less productive. Compromises are too easy to criticize in retrospect simply because the results everyone observes—often morally incoherent—are divorced from both the process and alternatives that were available at the time.

Political compromises, as we have seen, are usually a mélange of measures that reflect conflicting values that no set of moral standards can consistently encompass. The Tax Reform Act included exemptions and loopholes that violated principles that the president, along with leaders in the Senate and House, invoked to defend the ultimate compromise. Every health-care reform bill that had any chance of gaining a majority in Congress—let alone a filibuster-proof majority—also included measures that expressed conflicting values, such as maintaining fee-for-service provisions, exempting the most expensive employer health-care benefits from payroll taxes until 2018, and imposing cost controls on medical procedures. To judge compromises as acceptable only if they are consistent with a coherent standard is to put the compromise—but not the status quo—on the moral defensive.

A similar problem results from the most systematic attempt to seek coherence in legislation. The legal philosopher Ronald Dworkin defends an ideal of integrity in the law: "lawmakers [should] try to make the total set of laws morally coherent."[25] Integrity requires that a "compromise...be external, not internal; it must be a compromise about which scheme of justice to adopt rather than a compromised scheme of justice."[26] Yet integrity does not rule out all internal compromises: that would condemn almost all legislative compromises, because they typically combine parts of at least two schemes of justice that are not compatible with one another. But integrity, according to Dworkin, does rule out internal compromises that he calls "checkerboard compromises," in which a single principle is affirmed for one group but denied for another for no relevant moral reason.[27] In contrast, a compromise that orders or combines two different principles, such as a law prohibiting abortion except in the case of rape, does not violate integrity, even though it may be internally inconsistent from both the pro-life and pro-choice perspectives.[28]

As a moral guide, integrity may help to adjudicate some moral conflicts. Consider one of Dworkin's hypothetical examples. An opponent of the death penalty is faced with a choice between two compromises—both of which would reduce the total number of executions. One does so in a way that "those who are executed are morally more culpable than those who are not." Another reduces precisely as many executions but in a way that "allows some criminals convicted of a capital offense to escape death by drawing straws." The ideal of integrity would lead us to choose the first compromise and reject the drawing of straws to determine who lives and who does not. So might a well-specified principle of fairness, or nondiscrimination.[29]

The practical moral implication of Dworkin's arguments behind the capital punishment example is that the offenses punishable as capital crimes should not vary state by state, because that is the moral equivalent of allowing some criminals but not others to escape death by drawing straws. He uses the integrity argument to criticize controversial compromises across a very wide range of legislative action, ranging from setting strict liability standards on some product manufacturers but not others (without a morally relevant reason), to deferring to states to set abortion rights standards, to counting three-fifths of states' slaves for purposes of congressional representation.[30]

Using the integrity in the law as a moral guide, however, is very different from invoking it as a moral blockade to compromise. As a rigid rule, the integrity ideal would rule out all checkerboard compromises even if the only alternative were a status quo that was worse from the perspectives of all parties. "We say that a state that adopts these internal compromises," Dworkin writes, "is acting in an unprincipled way... [I]t is inconsistency in principle among the acts of the state personified that integrity *condemns*."[31]

Grant that the ideal of integrity captures something morally troubling in checkerboard legislation. It is still the case that an integrity ideal that condemns all checkerboard compromises, even those that turn out to be the only way to morally improve on the status quo, puts the state's action, not the status quo, on the defensive. In politics, state action is often required to maintain the status quo, which itself is usually the product of past compromises (or refusals to compromise). Dworkin cannot rest his integrity principle on a moral distinction between the ethics of action and inaction, especially because the principle explicitly invokes the idea of the state as a moral actor.

Just because attempts fail to distinguish in a principled way between acceptable and unacceptable compromises does not mean that principles are themselves unhelpful in politics. Quite the contrary: principles are an invaluable guide to the directions in which politicians should try to head in a compromise, and in which their supporters should want them to head. Everything we say here about the limits of principled tenacity is consistent with the importance of politicians and citizens guiding their judgments and actions by principles. The problem for democratic compromise—and democratic politics generally—arises when principles are treated not as a set of directional signals but rather as a series of roadblocks to compromises that would move society in the right direction, however imperfectly or partially.

Deliberative democratic theory is sometimes associated with taking principled stands in a way that might seem similar to principled tenacity. Indeed, deliberative theory emphasizes the value of principled arguments in politics. But many deliberative theorists now not only recognize but also insist on the need for, and value of, political compromise.[32] One of the defining features of deliberative democracy in our view—that its principles are provisional—places a limit on principled tenacity. The process of mutual reason-giving in deliberative democracy asks citizens and leaders to treat their principles as open to change. They should take seriously new evidence and arguments, and new interpretations of old evidence and arguments, including reasons offered by their opponents and reasons they may have rejected in the past.[33] This openness to change over time is a basis for the self-correcting capacity of deliberative democracy. It also helps to constrain the uncompromising mindset and promote desirable compromise.

Mutual Mistrust

The second characteristic of the uncompromising mindset—mutual mistrust—focuses on the attitude of the agents. Politicians with this mindset speak and act on the assumption that their opponents are motivated mainly by a desire to defeat them and the principles for which they stand.

The most common form of this mistrust is cynicism about the motives of both the proponents and opponents of any compromise—what we call motive cynicism. As the cynicism about the motives of politicians spreads to cynicism about the process of compromising, compromises become easier to resist and condemn.[34] When motives are mistrusted, suspicions that a better compromise could have been achieved come to the fore. Compromise is a fertile breeding ground for these suspicions because the process involves the interaction of conflicting wills that, unlike impersonal forces, are susceptible to modification. This creates a persistent hope on both sides that more could have been achieved if only one or the other had held out for more. It spawns continual mistrust of the motives of those who settled for less. At the extreme of mutual mistrust, total defeat of the opposition comes to seem the only means to an acceptable solution.

In the health-care debate, politicians of both parties continued in the campaign mode as they tried to legislate. The final bill could have been closer to the "ideal point" of Republican legislators if the moderates in the party had joined with the Democrats to forge a compromise. But the entire Republican delegation "held together, taking the risk of a bill with a stronger Democratic stance in return for gambling for the outcome they almost realized: *complete and total victory.*"[35]

Even in its earlier phases, when a bipartisan compromise did not seem out of the question, both sides reinforced their mutual mistrust by accusing each other of base motives. Health Care for America Now, a coalition of Democratic and labor groups, ran television commercials charging that Republican members of Congress (notably, House Minority Leader John Boehner) were opposed to changing health care because "they are in the pocket of the insurance companies and already have good coverage for themselves."[36] For his part, Boehner was not above questioning the motives of the Democrats' bill: "For whom was this bill actually written?...Is it really for the radical special interest and lobbying groups that invested millions to elect a cooperative president and Congress?"[37] Although the mutual disrespect reflected in these recriminations may not have been the main cause of the failure of bipartisan compromise, this kind of attack on motives is part of an uncompromising mindset that facilitates campaigning but frustrates cooperating across the aisle.

Motive cynicism comes from partisan supporters of politicians as much as from their adversaries. Politicians make campaign promises to their ardent supporters, but once elected, they find that they cannot fulfill them and have to compromise to get anything done. Their supporters accuse them of selling out, suspecting that they made the promises only to get elected. They are said to care more about holding on to power than honoring the promises they made in the campaign.

Recall George H. W. Bush's 1988 campaign promise: "Read my lips. No new taxes."[38] The promise shows the uncompromising mindset at work. In the campaign it served a legitimate strategic imperative: mobilize the base. It probably was a factor in Bush's victory, more clearly differentiating him from the Democratic opposition. Although politically convenient, the pledge to oppose tax increases was also consistent with his principles. There were no grounds for any specific suspicion about his motives beyond the general cynicism that many people often—and too easily—read into the conduct of all politicians who seek election.

Once in office, Bush repeatedly tried to cut spending rather than raise taxes as a means to reduce the growing national deficit, consistent with his campaign pledge. But he could make no headway with a Congress controlled by Democrats. Rather than let the budget expand even further, he ultimately agreed to a bipartisan compromise that raised several taxes as part of the 1990 budget agreement. His staunchest supporters felt betrayed more than did his partisan adversaries. His conservative challenger in the 1992 presidential primaries, Pat Buchanan, made effective use of Bush's promise-breaking, portraying him as a hypocritical, purely self-seeking politician. Later, in the general election, Bill Clinton used Bush's reversal on taxes to support the accusation that he was untrustworthy. Motive cynicism began to loom larger than policy criticism.

It is not easy to avoid the cynicism that the uncompromising mindset creates. If politicians never make campaign promises, their commitments are suspect, and their campaigns are likely to suffer. (Even if they "soften" promises with conditional qualifications, they are criticized for being noncommittal, and their campaigns are also hurt.) If they never break their promises, their compromises will be infrequent, and their efforts to improve the status quo are likely to falter.

After Bush's "read my lips" promise, many politicians have tried harder to avoid making such explicit pledges. But they still run on a general platform, they still express strong commitments and lofty goals, and they still fall short of achieving their campaign agenda and goals. When they take office and try to govern—with a compromising mindset—they are still vulnerable to charges that they have abandoned their strong campaign commitments, which were nourished by the uncompromising mindset.

Yet it is possible, even for the most competitive politician, to tame motive cynicism. At one of the many moments at which tax reform nearly collapsed in 1986, House Speaker Thomas "Tip" O'Neill stood as the only member with the power to allow a second vote on bringing the bill to the floor for a vote. A group of Republicans had defied their president and voted against bringing it to the floor the first time. O'Neill believed their motives were purely partisan, and for a while he considered retaliating by acting on his own partisan inclinations. The Democrats had done their part, and "if the bill failed now, there would be no one to blame but the Republicans."[39]

Had O'Neill retaliated, he would have become another exhibit in the pantheon of politicians who promote mutual mistrust. But he finally decided to trust the president to help put together enough Republican votes to allow the second vote to proceed and thus pass the bipartisan compromise. It is not that his motives were nobler than those of the Republicans. He may well have acted less out of regard for the public interest (or even partisan advantage) than respect for a personal aide and loyalty to Chairman Rostenkowski. The important point to notice is that setting aside mistrust of the motives of opponents, which may be necessary for continuing a negotiation, does not require politicians themselves to be nobly motivated.

To reach a compromise, politicians must adjust their wills as much as their reason. They must be able to set aside their mistrust of motives and to turn a will to oppose into a will to cooperate. That involves a psychological shift as much as a policy change. To avoid the spiral of mistrust that motive cynicism generates, democracy needs institutions that are designed to restrain the ascendancy of campaigning.

A recent defense of the Affordable Care Act against some progressive critics suggests that anyone who seeks more comprehensive reform should concentrate on changing the institutional facts of political life—including the filibuster, the accounting standards of the Congressional Budget Office, campaign financing, and the "awesome power of money in politics"—that "make the enactment of [more desirable] sweeping legislation nightmarishly difficult."[40] Making these institutional changes would count as comprehensive reform and would require precisely the kinds of broad-based compromises that tend to be blocked by the motive cynicism of the uncompromising mindset. A deeper appreciation of how destructive to democratic governance the dynamics of mutual mistrust can be, and how they are fueled by motive cynicism, is itself a necessary first step toward making almost any major institutional reform practically conceivable in democratic politics. But as we show later, such institutional reforms themselves require changes in the mindsets of politicians and citizens.

The politicians who supported the Tax Reform Act in 1986 were no nobler of motive than those who opposed it, but enough partisans on both sides overcame the tendency to think only the worst of their opponents. The opposite happened in the case of health care. The cynicism increased as the negotiations went on. The compromise that finally emerged required a shift in attitude about motives, but even then, it occurred only among some congressional Democrats toward one another.

Uncompromising Multiplied

Each of the two characteristics of the uncompromising mindset—principled tenacity and mutual mistrust—operating on its own can impede desirable legislation. They also can work in tandem. When they do, the effects are multiplied. Their interaction creates a cascade of intransigence.

The dynamic typically works this way. Both sides stake out their positions and declare that they will not compromise their principles. Moderates on each side come together to propose a compromise. The moderates are already at a disadvantage and their motives suspect because they have to admit that the compromise violates their principles (or, if they pretend otherwise, their critics will make the point in less kind terms). To build support for the compromise, the moderates need to win over some of those on each side who have declared their principled opposition to any concessions. They need only some, and they do not want too many. Because the compromise is not likely to be popular with the base on either side (especially in the coming campaign), even those who favor the compromise want only enough supporters to pass the legislation. Both want to maximize the number of converts from the other side, and minimize the number from their own side.

As a result, each side suspects the other of not recruiting enough supporters and of trying to gain electoral advantage. The maneuverings in this volatile mix of principled and strategic negotiation reinforce distrust, which in turn leads to more declarations of principle, which leads to more distrust, and on it goes. As the centrifugal elements of the uncompromising mindset continue to interact, the compromising center cannot hold. How this dynamic plays out in practice can be seen vividly in the process that led to the defeat of the Comprehensive Immigration Act of 2007.

Both parties agreed that U.S. policy on immigration urgently needed reform. Republicans were most concerned about the continuing flow of illegal immigrants to the United States. Democrats were more worried about the well-being of the estimated 12 million undocumented immigrants already in the country. Republicans argued as a matter of principle that they could not support any reform that would grant citizenship to people who had come to this country illegally. That would be amnesty—letting people who had committed a crime off the hook—and amnesty would be unjust. Democrats argued—also on the basis of a principle of justice—that immigration reform should not deny basic welfare and education to illegal immigrants, especially to their children. It should not exploit immigrants who are willing to do available work that Americans were unwilling to do.

After three bills had failed in earlier sessions of Congress, several members in both parties, represented by the so-called Gang of Twelve and with the support of President Bush, made another attempt. They proposed to provide undocumented immigrants a path to citizenship, boost border controls to stem the flow of illegal immigrants into the United States from Mexico, and establish a guest-worker program. The bill was a classic compromise, and it was deluged with moral criticism from both liberals and conservatives. Although illegal immigrants would be offered a new path to citizenship for the first time, citizenship would be far harder to obtain than liberals thought was fair. Illegal immigrants would need to pay fees, which many could not afford. While the guest worker program would allow more immigrants to enter the country, liberals argued that the program would create "a permanent underclass of imported workers to fill American jobs."[41] It would be unfair not only to the immigrants but also to American workers.

The critics on the conservative side were no happier with the bill. Supporting such a fatally flawed bill, they suggested, showed a willingness to sacrifice moral principles—"core values"—to political expediency.[42] President Bush tried to allay the critics' fears that the bill was a form of amnesty for illegal immigrants by emphasizing the bill's requirements that they pay fees and return home ("touchback") before being eligible for citizenship. But that defense just angered conservative critics more, who suspected that the supporters were selling out.[43]

Supporters of the bill were on the defensive against the majority of members of their own parties. As one observer noted, "[O]pponents passionately believe they are standing on principle, while proponents are 'holding their nose.'"[44] Against the backdrop of widespread and passionate opposition to compromise among so many politicians in both parties, it seemed that the best that they could say for this bill was that it was a necessary compromise. Given the opponents' attitude toward the very idea of compromise, this defense amounted to damning with perverse praise. "There is a lot in this bill I don't like very much. But I know that in order to get something, you have to give something," said Senator Jon Kyl, Republican of Arizona, one of the architects of the bill.[45] Senator Arlen Specter, Republican of Pennsylvania, spoke passionately in favor of compromise in general rather than this compromise in particular: "[T]his amendment was characterized by the Senator from New Mexico as the politics of compromise. Well, that might sound bad, but that happens to be the reality of what goes on in the Senate all the time. It goes on in all political bodies ... [T]here is nothing inappropriate about the politics of compromise. That means we sacrifice the better for the good."[46]

Had the backdrop of this debate differed, the proponents might have been more effective in countering the principled attacks with prudent appeals to sacrificing "the better for the good." After all, most politicians—even those who profess to be standing firm on principle—are not principled purists. But the debate and negotiations had reinforced the distrust already brewing within and between the parties. As these negotiations proceeded, principled stands interacted with motive cynicism, each intensifying the other at nearly every stage.

In the earliest stage, the compromise was negotiated by a small group of senators operating behind closed doors. Although secrecy may have been necessary at the beginning (as often is the case with political compromises), the clandestine origins of this deal increased the critics' suspicions about the motives of those proposing it. This made the need for public explanation greater once the proposal reached the floor. But instead the leaders sought to limit debate, fueling the mistrust. "This agreement was reached between a handful of senators," said Senator Jeff Bingaman of New Mexico, one of the Democrats who balked and voted against limiting debate. "That should not be considered a substitute for deliberation by the full Senate."[47] This step in the process made the compromise look even less principled, and the motives of its supporters more suspect. Every tactical step, thought necessary for the bill to have a chance to pass, instead extends the cycle of cynicism.

The tactics of the opponents of the compromise raised questions about just how principled they were as well. Some voted against an amendment that improved the chances that the bill would pass even though they had voted for essentially the same amendment just a few days before. Their vote raised "questions about their intent to stall the bill."[48] One of the senators who voted against the amendment, Jim DeMint of South Carolina, admitted that was "part of his motivation ... If this vote helped to derail it, I would support it."[49] As the process went forward, the debate became even more acrimonious. Members began to resist normally routine requests.[50] "We are in trench warfare," said Senator Specter, who strongly supported the bill.[51]

Although the election was more than a year away, the campaign mentality intruded, fomenting discord even among senators who supported the compromise. Senator Lindsey Graham, a South Carolina Republican who had championed the compromise, and Barack Obama, then a Democratic senator who ultimately voted with Graham, exchanged verbal blows on the floor and continued their quarrel in the press. Graham accused Obama of "playing presidential politics because he proposed a change that key negotiators said would tank the bill and undercut senators, particularly Republicans, who have endured harsh criticism for supporting it."[52] Graham spoke directly to Obama: "So when you're out on the campaign trail, my friend, tell them about why we can't come together ... This is why."[53]

The uncompromising mindset so evocative of electoral campaigning showed itself in other ways as well. In the House, Democratic leaders, lukewarm in their support of the bill, insisted that Republicans deliver at least sixty votes, preferably more, so that freshman Democrats from marginal districts could go on record against it.[54] Senator John McCain put his nomination prospects at risk by cosponsoring the legislation with Senator Ted Kennedy. Presidential rival Rudolph Giuliani castigated him for saying that the bill had not been everything he would have wanted. Taking the uncompromising stance, Giuliani hectored him: "Then he should have written the one he wanted and pushed that."[55] Later in the primary, under the pressure of continuing criticism for his role in the compromise, McCain abandoned his support for any comprehensive reform.

The Senate never voted on the bill itself. Supporters failed to get the sixty votes needed to end debate. Thirty-seven Republicans joined with fifteen Democrats and one Independent to sustain the filibuster, 53–46. The vote doomed this compromise and dashed the hopes for any comprehensive immigration reform. Supporters "hoped for a bipartisan accomplishment [but] what we got was a bipartisan defeat."[56]

The parties now moved openly into the campaign mode. The day after the vote, Majority Leader Reid issued a statement declaring: "Republicans torpedoed comprehensive immigration reform."[57] Republicans fired back: Reid never really had "embraced the bill and had … set up Republicans to take the fall."[58] The Democratic proponents of the compromise insisted that they had "done more than [their] share" to round up votes from their reluctant colleagues, and they doubted that Republican proponents had done the same. The Republican supporters made similar claims and expressed similar suspicions about their erstwhile Democratic allies. Congressional staffers who had worked on the bill for months believed that this mutual mistrust was the "*mindset* that helped contribute to the failure."[59]

In retrospect, it seems clear that too many forces were working against the compromise and too few pressing for it. Failure had many faces, and nearly all displayed themselves in the uncompromising mindset that informed the debate and undermined the negotiations. Principled tenacity and mutual mistrust, cumulatively reinforcing each other in a cascade of intransigence, combined to crush the efforts of the precarious coalition of compromisers.

The casualties of this episode were not only the hope for reform but also the spirit of compromise. Yet the possibility of compromise never disappears completely from the democratic process. The proponents of compromise have resources of their own, as we can see by examining more closely the mindset that seeks compromise.

3

SEEKING COMPROMISE

Some politicians are willing to defend compromise—and implicitly the mindset that seeks it. Consider this excerpt from *Time* editor Belinda Luscombe's interview with former Republican Senator Alan Simpson on the subject of the debt-ceiling compromise:

LUSCOMBE: What's the biggest obstacle to cutting the deficit?

SIMPSON: The absolute rigidity of the parties. I've never seen that before. Somebody said they're as rigid as a fireplace poker but without the occasional warmth.

...

LUSCOMBE: If you were in office today, would you sign Grover Norquist's no-tax pledge?

SIMPSON: Hell, no! Why would you sign anything before you went into office or before you had the debate and listened to it?

LUSCOMBE: Well, obviously, to get elected?

SIMPSON: I never signed it, and I never got defeated for re-election. The revenue coming into the U.S. [government] is 15% of GDP, which is the lowest since the Korean War. In the past 20 years, it has been 19% to 20%. If you can't move that a half-inch, then you're never going to get anywhere.[1]

At the same time, Simpson affirmed the need for legislators to seek compromise, not only in the debate over the deficit but more generally. "If you can't learn to compromise on an issue without compromising yourself," Simpson said in no uncertain terms, "then you shouldn't be a legislator."[2]

To serve the purpose of governing, the compromising mindset turns the defining characteristics of political compromise—mutual sacrifice and willful opposition—in a more constructive direction than does the uncompromising mindset. The compromising mind sees mutual sacrifice as an occasion neither to hold tenaciously to principles nor to abandon them merely to reach agreement. Rather, it regards mutual sacrifice as an opportunity to adjust principles in order to improve on the status quo. This is what we have called principled prudence. In the second defining characteristic, willful opposition, the compromising mindset finds, not an excuse for mistrust or cynicism about motives, but rather a resource for promoting greater understanding and accommodation among those who disagree. This is the aim of mutual respect.

Together, principled prudence and mutual respect increase the chances that the general value of compromise will play a role in judging particular compromises and that desirable compromises will be recognized as such.

Principled Prudence

The politician guided by principled prudence begins with the pragmatic recognition that compromise is usually necessary in a democracy to accomplish anything of significance. But principled prudence amounts to more than making a virtue out of necessity. It has a moral component: to fail to compromise in politics is to privilege the status quo. If a compromise is likely to be an improvement, then a compromising mindset opens up opportunities to promote greater justice.

Although (as we argued in chapter 2) a single set of coherent principles cannot capture the overall value of a compromise, it is still necessary to decide whether a compromise is better than the status quo. That is the minimal condition for defending any compromise. It requires showing that the compromise is an improvement from the perspectives of all parties to the agreement. Otherwise, the agreement is not a compromise but a capitulation by one side to the other.

The judgment that a compromise is an improvement is in principle contestable, sometimes reasonably so.

But in practice the objection that a particular compromise is worse than nothing is often disingenuous. It serves as a common tactic in the bargaining process. When the objection rests on a genuine comparison between the compromise and the status quo, it often assumes the possibility of achieving a better compromise in the foreseeable future. In that case, the objection is not that the proposed compromise itself is worse than the status quo, but that it is worse than a hoped-for future compromise. This was the logic behind many of the Republican objections to the Democrats' health-care reform bills. After the U.S. senatorial election in Massachusetts that broke the Democrats' supermajority in 2010, John Boehner, then House minority leader, commented: "They are still trying to find a way to shove this down the throats of the American people... Let's *start over* on common sense steps that we can take to make our system work better."[3]

One problem with rejecting a compromise in the hope of a better one to come is that the rejection itself becomes an obstacle to reaching the future compromise. In this case, "starting over" was not a plausible prescription for achieving a bipartisan compromise, because of the polarized politics of the Congress and the uncompromising mindsets that prevailed there. The political forces in play were signaling an even greater unwillingness to compromise later.

In all cases, the judgment about whether a particular compromise is worse than a hypothetical future compromise depends on an assessment of the political forces in play. Those assessments are generally colored by partisan views of the content of the compromises in question. The effect that rejecting a current compromise has on relationships among the parties, and their inclination to trust one another enough to engage in serious negotiations in the future, does not usually receive due consideration in the assessment.

The compromising mindset cannot eliminate all of these biases, but it can help clarify the value of the current compromise by directing attention to the essential comparison. The key question remains: is the proposal better than the status quo? Principled prudence also reminds us that the status quo guarantees neither stability nor improvement. Indeed, accepting the status quo can lead directly to change that no one wants.

Principled prudence reverses the uncompromising perspective on the incoherence of compromises. It sees the incoherence of the principles underlying most compromises—the Tax Reform Act, for example, which as a whole was inconsistent with any single set of principles—as a sign of success. Such incoherence can indicate that the democratic process respects competing principles and values. If the process has been fair and the outcome an improvement, then disarray in the principles should at least be appreciated, if not celebrated.

Principled prudence should not be mistaken for being unprincipled. Some of the most successful compromisers are as well known for taking strong, principled stands as they are for making difficult compromises. By the end of his time in Congress, Senator Ted Kennedy was respected as a legislative leader who stood on principle but could adapt his principles when necessary to reform current policy in the direction that his core values dictated. His role in health-care reform is a case in point. When he compromised, he had more credibility to defend the proposal to his allies. He had the standing to say that this is the best we can get, and he was able to provide cover for those in his party who might otherwise be accused of selling out.

While principled prudence counsels taking a positive attitude toward compromise, it does not require that compromises be defended as such. Politicians proclaim their belief in the general value of compromise, but they may still try to avoid acknowledging that a particular agreement is in fact a compromise. They prefer to present it as a victory for their uncompromising supporters. Many supporters of the Tax Reform Act defended it as a win for their side—which it was, as it also was for their partisan opposition. This tactic is prudent, provided that it is accompanied by a continuing commitment to seek compromises in the future.

One of the masters of legislative compromise, Lyndon Johnson, combined a strong defense of compromise in general with an equally strong defense of his particular deals as something other than compromises. Recall that Johnson considered himself "a consensus man."[4] By most accounts, this self-description was quite accurate and reflected his natural political dispositions. But when it came to defending a particular compromise, such as the Civil Rights Act of 1964, Johnson steered clear of calling it a compromise. To avoid prolonging a filibuster in the Senate, Johnson had accepted an amendment that weakened the House bill by limiting the government's power to regulate private business. The act fell short of what he had proposed and had hoped to achieve. Rather than acknowledging the concessions, he portrayed the result as an out-and-out victory.[5]

Johnson's speeches celebrating the Civil Rights Act suggested that a great historic advance had been achieved—as indeed it had been. Even so, some of his liberal allies strongly believed that significantly more could have been attained if he had not conceded so much. They suspected him of selling out. His compromising mindset no doubt helped produce a major improvement on the status quo. Yet—as must be expected in compromises—the uncompromising criticisms from both left and right continued. Politicians with compromising mindsets recognize that opposition to particular compromises will often persist, because their supporters' expectations almost always outstrip the capacity of even the most skillful politicians to deliver. In face of criticism, they understandably want to claim victory. The compromising mindset need not always label its products as compromises.

But would it not be better if politicians explicitly recognized particular compromises for what they are? That
might help give compromise a better name. It might
facilitate compromises in the future. And it would be
a small step toward greater political candor. At some
points in the process of negotiation, compromises must
be recognized as such, because of the nature of the support they need and the opposition they engender. But
explicit acknowledgment all the time is neither a moral
imperative nor a service to the cause of compromise.
For those in the grip of principled tenacity, the plea
to vote for a bill as a compromise is more of a reason
to vote against it than for it. Recall that Senator Arlen
Specter did not merely defend the 2007 immigration
bill as a compromise against the accusation that it was
an example of "the politics of compromise." He also
defended the compromise, in the spirit of principled
prudence, as on balance "good" compared to the status
quo.[6] Rather than dwelling on its being a compromise,
principled prudence counsels showing why a bill is
worth supporting on the merits.

When does principled prudence counsel that a compromise is acceptable? In the previous chapter we suggested that it is a mistake to use absolute principles to
make such decisions, or to let principles prevent any
modifications in positions in the process of compromising. But the compromising mindset does not leave
the decision to compromise completely open. Quite
the contrary, principled prudence advises us to use

principled considerations as guides both in deciding whether to compromise and in judging compromises.

To see how this might work, we can take some cues from John Stuart Mill, whose conception of compromise was refined in the contentious cauldron of nineteenth-century British parliamentary politics. Mill developed a set of considerations that he believed should be taken into account in deciding whether to attempt to compromise and whether to accept a particular compromise.[7] A compromise is morally defensible insofar as the time is not ripe to realize the measure your own side prefers, your opponents' position contains something worthy, the agreement would not set back progress already made, and it would facilitate future cooperation. He added a novel but important further condition: the compromise should "embody or recognize" the principle that you are trying to realize, even if it falls short of doing so. The principle that all adults have a right to a voice in government is recognized in a compromise that increases the size of the adult male electorate (for example, by dropping the requirement that citizens must be property owners) even though the compromise excludes most women, and thereby perpetuates what Mill himself considered a major injustice.

Mill treated all these criteria as factors to be considered in assessing particular political compromises. They express values to be weighed against other values in reaching an all-things-considered judgment about any particular compromise in comparison with the status quo. Although this way of thinking about compromise is in keeping with a consequentialist approach, it is not distinctively tied to one. It is compatible with judging whether the status quo or available compromises better recognize human rights, dignity, and other nonconsequentialist values. Moreover, nonconsequentialist theories, like consequentialist ones, recognize that public officials—having accepted a public trust—are responsible not only for harming others (actions) but also for failing to aid others (omissions). The distinction between action and omission does not excuse public officials if they fail to compromise when they should, any more than if they compromise when they should not.

For public officials, the refusal to improve a society when the status quo entails the perpetuation of harm, the denial of rightful benefits, or the violation of human rights is the moral equivalent of needlessly harming or denying people their deserved benefits or their basic rights. This is so because public officials—unlike private individuals—cannot credibly deny their primary and direct responsibility for securing the well-being of their society, according to some combination of their own and their constituents' best moral lights. The support by public officials of the status quo, in refusing to compromise, has the same moral weight as their agreement to compromise. No theory of justice should give public officials a presumptive moral discount for omissions.

The complex and continuing nature of lawmaking also allows less scope for absolutist judgments than do typical two-party, one-time interactions, but it still leaves plenty of scope for principled moral judgments. The compromising mindset makes context-sensitive judgments, modifying and balancing principles as appropriate and declining to depend on any general rule that purports to fit all legislative circumstances. That is the counsel of principled prudence.

Mutual Respect

The second characteristic of the compromising mindset confronts the willful opposition embodied in political compromises. It tells adversaries to negotiate in good faith and to restrain suspicions about ulterior motives. Assume that your opponents' motives are mixed, that they act not only for their own political gain but also out of a desire to do what they think is right. Mutual respect seeks to counter the motive cynicism cultivated by the mutual mistrust in the uncompromising mindset.

At the same time, mutual respect expresses an orientation toward the political process that sees politicians as colleagues who can work together in the enterprise of governing, and more generally as citizens bound together under a common constitution. Political adversaries who respect each other argue and negotiate in the belief that they might join together to support a particular compromise that is on balance good, even if it is not what they would enact on their own, and—like democracy itself—is inevitably far from perfect.

Like toleration, mutual respect is a form of agreeing to disagree, but mutual respect goes beyond the "live and let live" attitude that toleration promotes. Mutual respect expresses a constructive attitude toward, and interaction with, the persons with whom one disagrees. It is the mindset of individuals who enter into negotiations in good faith, presuming their adversaries are as well motivated as they are, and are trying to act at least partly on principle to accomplish what they believe is politically good for society.

Negotiations informed by mutual respect approximate what has been called a "moralized compromise procedure." Such a procedure "filters out" factors that undermine mutual respect.[8] In a perfect good faith negotiation, the agreement would not be determined by such factors as "the relative position of the disputing parties, their ability to bluff (e.g., pretend to hold a more extreme view than they in fact do, so that a compromise will fall closer to the position they actually hold), the ability of a party to hold out longer, and differences in who needs agreement more (because the status quo without an agreement on a government policy favors one view rather than another)."[9] In politics, these factors of course are always present, but the less influence they have, the more the process is primed to support mutual respect. Ideally, mutual respect also includes keeping open the possibility of changing one's mind about the means or ends of a proposed policy, and even about the framework for negotiation.[10] Staying alert to this possibility is a desirable component of the compromising mindset but not a necessary condition for manifesting it.

Mutual respect can clearly benefit democratic politics. It is a virtue that makes debate more civil and relations more collegial. But it is more than that. In the case of compromise, it plays a special, more direct political role. For parties to accept a compromise, they (and their supporters) have to believe that they are getting as much as they can reasonably expect under the circumstances. They do not want to sacrifice their principles or disappoint their supporters by passing up a better result they could have won if they had put more pressure on their adversaries or held out for more concessions. The absence of mutual respect blocks compromise by reinforcing the motive cynicism that lurks in the hearts of both politicians and voters.

The biggest challenge in defending an attitude of respect toward adversaries arises from the fact that the parties to a legislative compromise rarely, if ever, can be certain that an agreement is the best they could achieve under the circumstances. This uncertainty infects not only ex-ante but also ex-post judgments about compromises. The answer to the question of what would have happened if one's own side had resisted more strongly depends on a complex set of counterfactual assumptions that are hard to assess objectively either during or after the process of compromising. People are more certain about their principles than they are about probabilities, and judgment therefore tends to be driven more by principles. This dynamic also reinforces principled tenacity against principled prudence.

Under conditions of uncertainty, the trust that mutual respect generates is therefore essential. It is one of the few resources on which the parties to a compromise can draw to assure themselves that they are getting as much as they can reasonably expect, and to convince their supporters that they are not selling out. If you and your supporters have reason to believe that your adversary is negotiating in good faith, you can have more confidence in deciding whether and how much to concede. If you and your supporters suspect that your adversaries are engaged in duplicitous behavior, you are likely to resist a compromise even if it appears to be (and actually is) an improvement on the status quo. By the same token, compromise becomes more difficult to the extent that adversaries try to take advantage of the vulnerabilities of the other side, manipulate public opinion, or threaten political reprisals out of proportion to the issues at stake. Without mutual trust in the background, even the normal practices of legislative negotiation—such as avoiding premature disclosure of your willingness to compromise or the final terms you would accept—are likely to raise suspicion and undermine cooperation.

The cynical attitude that looks for ulterior motives in every move by political opponents is of course not entirely wrong. Most politicians want to win and hold office, please their constituents, and advance their careers. It would be not only surprising but also disturbing if they lacked these political motives. But it is almost completely useless to make a point of exposing one of these motives behind every stand a politician takes, if there is nothing of substance to be said about the politician's position. Potentially, when this cynical attitude is reinforced by media coverage, it undermines constructive political action (as we discuss in chapter 5). The motives of politicians, like most people in responsible positions, are mixed. It is hardly news to report that politicians are acting politically.

To be sure, the process of compromise supplies more than enough evidence for motive cynicism. Early in the debate about health-care reform in 2009, Senator Jim DeMint of South Carolina urged his fellow Republicans to work against any reform so that the Democrats would suffer political losses. "If we're able to stop Obama on this, it will be his Waterloo. It will break him."[11] Even if few of his colleagues followed him, his call for all-out opposition served to strengthen the hands of the cynics who believed that the opposition was purely politically motivated. It also weakened the already wavering will of those with a more compromising mindset who were hoping to craft a bipartisan compromise on health-care reform.

Even worthy attempts to keep reaching out to opponents who persistently rebuff your approaches need not be driven mainly by noble motives. If opponents are unwilling to concede anything of importance, this approach may still offer valuable moral and political cover when you finally have to draw the line and reject a putative compromise that would actually amount to a capitulation. President Obama's first chief of staff, Rahm Emanuel, seemed to have something like this in mind when he claimed that members of the administration could genuinely say that they had tried for bipartisanship in health-care reform, but they were not met halfway: "The public wants bipartisanship...We just have to try. We don't have to succeed."[12] The attempt was not entirely wholehearted. The Democrats spurned at least one of the Republicans' plausible offers—cooperation on tort reform. Nor was it without political intent: "I don't think the onus is on us. We tried. The story is they [the Republicans] failed."[13] Cynics will find nothing but political maneuvering going on here, and it certainly was going on—as it almost always is in politics.

Nevertheless, by reaching out to opponents, politicians also cultivate relationships that can be politically productive over time and conducive to good governance. With these overtures, they also make an important symbolic statement and keep open the possibility of cooperation on the basis of mutual respect. Whatever their intentions, they may find that their opponents even take them up on their offer. If it turns out that their opponents still show no willingness to compromise, they can take the high ground by demonstrating that they are not the ones blocking cooperation. Mutual respect can be good politics as well as good government.

The window of compromise rarely opens to politicians who always assume the worst about the motives of their adversaries. It takes repeated outreach to adversaries, accompanied by at least a temporary suspension of motive cynicism, to discover opportunities for compromise. This is especially true with comprehensive measures like those of tax reform. President Reagan approached Democrats as well as Republicans in order to pull off the compromise that became the Tax Reform Act. So did Dan Rostenkowski, who worked closely with receptive members of both parties on his House Ways and Means Committee. Political motives were at work in both cases, but the leaders did not dwell on them.

A striking illustration can be found in Senator Bob Packwood's decision to drop his opposition to tax reform in 1986 and the reactions of his colleagues to his shift on the issue. When he decided to support reform, he must have calculated that continued opposition to a successful bill would jeopardize his chances for reelection at a time when his party's popular president had made tax reform a chief domestic initiative for his second term. It would have been easy—and not inaccurate—for both supporters and critics of the compromise to challenge Packwood's motives. He could have been portrayed as interested only in reelection and as hypocritical for abandoning his long-standing opposition to reform. "On taxes," he had once said, "I'm as predictable as the sun rising." He had by his own account always been "a big [tax] credit man."[14] Yet he decided to partner with Democratic Senator Bill Bradley to pass tax reform in the Senate—championing a bill based on the House's version, which many Republicans in the House had declined to support. According to Bradley's admiring account, Packwood "became a fearsome and effective supporter of tax reform."[15] The bipartisan support for this measure probably would have broken down had motive cynicism rather than mutual respect dominated the tax-reform process.[16]

The kind of broad-based mutual respect that emerged in the negotiations over the Tax Reform Act is more naturally cultivated in governing than in campaigning (as we discuss further in the next chapter). In governing, it can produce legislative results—if all goes well. In campaigning, it is not as useful as motive cynicism in producing electoral results—if all goes as usual. A campaign is a competitive, zero-sum activity. Defeating your adversary is the dominant and legitimate motive. The more campaign attitudes infiltrate the legislative process, the less scope there is for mutual respect. Because campaigning fuels motive cynicism, it needs to be tempered to allow mutual respect to emerge and effective governing to take place. A robust governing process in turn provides defenses against motive cynicism.

Economizing on Disagreement

The compromising mindset is strengthened when politicians adopt a more accommodating style of politics— what we call economizing on disagreement.[17] In its original form, economizing on disagreement expresses the idea that citizens and their representatives should defend their preferred proposals in a way that minimizes rejecting the positions they oppose. The basis for recommending this approach as a strategy for governing is partly instrumental. The assumption is that following it increases the chances of producing a desirable compromise and thereby creating the conditions for cooperation that lead to future compromises. But no less important, the approach also affirms a moral commitment to democratic cooperation and manifests the value of mutual respect.

Applying the economy of disagreement to legislative politics, we broaden its scope. Economizing on disagreement takes the form of a variety of practices, extending beyond rationales for laws to include the actions, attitudes, and arguments of lawmakers. To illustrate how the approach might work in legislative politics, we describe several strategies of accommodation that could fortify the compromising mindset and foster desirable compromises. In the next chapter, we discuss institutional and other incentives that could help sustain these and similar practices.

SEPARATING THE ISSUES

Legislators can try to reach agreement by dividing issues into more and less contentious parts and then make a deal on the less contentious parts as a way to build mutual trust for finding agreement on the more contentious ones. This strategy worked in 2009 when both parties put aside their differences on health-care reform to pass a vast expansion of children's health insurance.[18] The strategy of separating the issues is valuable when available, but of limited use when a more comprehensive policy change is sought and many issues need to be combined. In the case of more sweeping proposals for health-care reform, the less and the more contentious parts of the agenda are closely interconnected and often even essential to the reform sought, and they cannot be effectively uncoupled. Even the idea of separation may be controversial—for example, whether a requirement of mandatory health-care coverage can be detached from the provisions intended to control costs.

A more promising strategy of separation in many cases is to seek cooperation on different but related issues on which there might be more hope for agreement.

Even those who disagree about abortion may still agree on the importance of providing pregnant teenage girls the support they may want and need to become mothers. The abortion compromise in the health-care debate was much more limited, consisting mainly of an agreement not to adopt anything that would change the current law.

A variation on this strategy does not set aside the separate issue but rather brings a new issue into the negotiations. Tax bills offer many opportunities for introducing measures that had not previously been thought to be part of the discussions. When used constructively, the strategy can correct an apparent imbalance in a compromise—for example, by adjusting completely different taxes that were not originally under consideration.

Finally, compromises on separate issues that are not very closely related to those in the disputed compromise can improve the climate of negotiation and strengthen mutual respect. Even as the parties continued their contentious debate about health care in early 2010, Congress managed briefly to pass a modestly bipartisan bill intended to create jobs, a goal that both shared. The flame of mutual respect did not shine brightly or for long, but it sent a much-needed signal that cooperation is not impossible.

The governing process is more likely to encourage mutual respect through this other-issue type of cooperation to the extent that it takes place in institutions that require politicians to work together on a continuing basis and that permits them to develop reputations and cultivate relationships across oppositional divides. Trust is less likely to be generated in single-issue negotiations than in continuing interactions over time, as politicians who oppose one another on some issues find ways to work together on others.

As mistrust can degenerate into a spiral of suspicion that is hard to stop, so trust, once established, is self-reinforcing.[19] It can persist even in the face of strong disagreements and ideological polarization. In the presence of mutual respect (along with principled prudence), the strong ideological differences that characterize a polarized politics need not stand in the way of cooperation.

The collaborations of Senators Orrin Hatch and Ted Kennedy illustrate the potential of mutual respect and trust developed over time. Despite standing on the right and left wings of their parties, they managed "to come together in a bipartisan fashion to craft some of this nation's most important health legislation."[20] During the nearly two decades in which they alternated as either chairman or ranking member of the Senate committee concerned with health care, education, and labor issues, they cosponsored many significant legislative initiatives, including measures that provided support for victims of AIDS, created the children's health insurance program, and established protections against discrimination toward individuals with disabilities.

DEFUSING THE AGENDA

Legislators carry a brimful bag of tricks that they use to try to control the agenda to the disadvantage of their opponents. Some examples: proposing bills on hot-button issues of less importance with no chance of passage, merely for the purpose of mobilizing the base; presenting only criticisms with no constructive alternatives; and inserting provisions in a bill that force its proponents to vote no (so-called poison pills). Many of these tactics are part and parcel of conventional politics. But under some circumstances they also stand in the way of desirable compromise and befoul the climate for agreement in the future.

Both parties have deployed all of these tactics at various times. When, in 2005, President Bush began to try to deal with the proverbial third rail of U.S. politics, Social Security reform, the Democrats did not put forth any serious alternatives because they were more interested in developing the "mind-set of an opposition."[21] While the Republicans mostly controlled both the House and the Senate in the same period, Tom DeLay, the Republican leader in the House, liked to "lace bills with poison pill provisions so unpopular with core Democratic groups that even Democrats sympathetic to the overall legislation could not vote for them."[22] He used the tactic on many different issues, ranging from a drug bill to trade legislation. His aim evidently was to force moderate Democrats to cast a vote that would be unpopular with powerful business interests in their districts, which could then be used against them in the campaign.[23]

From the perspective of each party, it is easy to understand why these tactics seemed warranted. The possibilities for working together were already limited, and the only alternative seemed to be to look to the next campaign with the hope of strengthening their own numbers. But in a continuing institution like a legislature, in which the control shifts from time to time, members can reasonably assume that methods they use against the opposition will be used against them later. Some observers commented that Nancy Pelosi was just using the same tactics that Newt Gingrich had used against the Democrats twenty years earlier (significantly, against the advice of Bob Michel, the moderate Republican and longtime minority leader in the House).[24] If twenty years is not enough to break a mutually destructive cycle of mistrust, then the cascade of intransigence is likely to continue.

A never-ending cascade need not be inevitable. It is possible to establish rules that discourage some of these tactics, or at least to reserve them for exceptional circumstances. In any case, greater publicity about how these tactics are used and with what effect on the public interest could serve as a deterrent. The media—and partly as a consequence, the public—do not pay enough attention to the important question of how the political agenda is shaped, and the many ways in which it can be, and too often is, manipulated so as to block the possibilities for productive compromise.

RESTRAINING THE RHETORIC

A third strategy of economizing on disagreement is designed to deal with the fact that disagreement will persist on most issues. The democratic process does not always or even usually yield agreement, let alone general consensus. Dealing with the disagreement that is endemic to democratic politics in a respectful way is essential to reaching desirable compromises, whether in the present or the future. This strategy recognizes that rhetoric makes a difference. How politicians describe the substance of the proposals they oppose and the motives of the colleagues proposing them affects the possibility of mutual respect. Economizing requires a specific kind of verbal self-restraint in politics: it counsels avoidance of extreme exaggeration of the positions of opponents.

Some Republican opponents of the Democratic proposal to fund end-of-life counseling claimed that the program created "death panels," implying that the Democrats' proposal would force euthanasia on the infirm elderly.[25] They may have succeeded in temporarily obstructing the health-care reform process, but they also demonstrated such disrespect for their opponents that they lost the respect of some potential allies. The vice chair of the Senate Republican Conference set a better tone: "It does us no good to incite fear in people by saying that there's these end-of-life provisions, these death panels...Quite honestly, I'm so offended at that terminology because it absolutely isn't [in the bill]. There is no reason to gin up fear in the American public by saying things that are not included in the bill."[26]

Economizing also disfavors extreme exaggerations of your own position. Some hyperbole is of course to be expected in any negotiation. In a political negotiation, public officials are not expected to make their last, best offer their first offer. But taking absolute stands even when they know they are likely to back down does not create the best climate for good faith negotiation. If their opponents respond in kind, the chances of deadlock are increased. If they (or their opponents) do back down, credibility and therefore mutual trust are weakened. When the actual positions of some politicians lie at the far end of the political spectrum, their sincere declarations may be mistaken as extreme exaggerations. But to the extent that the politicians have track records, and develop long-term relationships with colleagues, it is usually possible to distinguish extreme exaggeration from an extreme position. Neither is helpful for reaching compromises, but the former strikes more directly at mutual respect.

Some liberal Democrats insisted that a public option must be part of any health-care reform. This was an acceptable tactic if the aim was to put pressure on their leaders to hold out for as much as possible. But if the president and the majority of the Democratic members had made the public option a deal breaker, there would have been no health-care reform bill. Drawing lines in the sand may sometimes be a useful tactic, but if it is used routinely or indiscriminately by those who seek compromise, it is likely to be counterproductive.

When politicians elevate their position to the level of a theory or ideology, this may or may not be an exaggeration, but it often has the same effect. When a disagreement is portrayed as a clash of capitalism and socialism, or liberalism and conservatism, or even egalitarianism and libertarianism, the scope for compromise is immediately curtailed. Let the writers of think pieces and the philosophers of politics put the disagreements in elevated perspectives if they wish. But it is better if the politicians stay closer to the ground and argue about particular points in particular laws.[27]

REFINING THE PARTISANSHIP

In the 1950s, an influential report by a committee of the American Political Science Association (APSA) criticized the two major parties for not being partisan enough.[28] The system offered voters no clear choices, or as some said, a choice only between "tweedledum and tweedledee." The committee's main message was that citizens need sharply differentiated parties not only so that they have clear choices when they go to the polls but also so that the party that wins can be held responsible for governing in a way that reflects those choices. One implication was that bipartisanship and compromise, if carried too far, undermine political responsibility.

Subsequent political history reminds us that these goals—sharp partisan differences and greater political responsibility—do not necessarily go together. A more clearly defined difference between the parties did not lead to more responsible party government in the way that the APSA committee hoped. The committee understandably failed to anticipate the realignment of southern Democrats with the Republicans, the rise of the Republican Right, and the growing extremism of both parties' bases. As the parties polarized, the extreme differences made it less likely that either could be seen as responsible to the median voter. The lesson some commentators draw from the efforts to sharpen the differences between the parties is "beware of what you wish for."[29]

The democratic process depends on vigorous contestation, and partisanship is no doubt essential to sustaining it. Any defense of compromise must make room for contestation. The compromising mindset is completely compatible with partisanship—at least with what has been called "respectable partisanship."[30] The best defenses of partisanship expect that partisans will act in ways that are consistent with principled prudence and mutual respect. Responsible partisans advance principles they believe others could share, strive to "locate

common ground," and are "as ready to peacefully suffer [their] losses as to enjoy [their] victories."[31]

A compelling defense of parties and partisanship by
the political theorist Nancy Rosenblum identifies the
"disposition to compromise" as one of only three essential qualities that partisans must have if partisanship is
to serve democratic politics well.[32] It is important that
partisans display this disposition toward their "fellow
partisans" as well as "across the aisle."[33] Compromise
both within and across parties is essential to enabling
democracy to work in a way that realizes partisanship's
ultimate purpose of good governance. The "ethics of
partisanship" rejects "uncompromising extremism" because it lacks a "commitment to getting the public business done" and represents an "abdication of responsibility for governing."[34]

Even in opposition a party bears some responsibility
for governing. Responsible opposition would call for a
more refined partisanship than Speaker Nancy Pelosi
promoted at times during George W. Bush's presidency.
According to observers, she discouraged Democrats
from cosponsoring bills with Republicans and ranking
Democrats from negotiating with their counterparts on
legislation as it moved through the various committees.
Why? Because they "might later use the Democratic
support to tout their commitment to bipartisanship
during their reelection campaigns."[35] Unrefined partisanship shuns the strategy of economizing on partisan
disagreement.

Most congressional Republicans in this period were at least as unrefined in their partisanship. In 2003, the Senate passed a prescription drug bill with overwhelming support from both parties. But when the bill went to the conference committee, only two Democrats were included, both known to be more conservative on this issue. The result was a final bill that tilted heavily toward the more conservative House version and a final vote that was blatantly partisan. Some Democrats believed that the Republicans "were calibrating the final product to minimize the number of Democrats who could support it so that the GOP could claim sole credit for the program."[36] Even some Republicans began to see a pattern: "It seems over the last couple of years [that] if something can come to the floor and you can pass it with a bipartisan majority ... or you can bring it to the floor in a way that you can just get Republican support and use it as a political issue against the Democrats, we have chosen the latter every time."[37] The costs of such unrefined partisanship are considerable— opportunities missed for making progress that could benefit many citizens.

Partisanship is both a necessary and a desirable feature of democratic politics. The partisanship that is worth defending is the kind practiced by those who are prepared to make prudent but principled concessions and are ready to contend vigorously but respectfully with their opponents in order to get the public's business done. The compromising mindset lets parties maintain their distinctive identities and to press their partisan agendas vigorously, not only in campaigning, but also in governing. Otherwise, little would be left to compromise. But it also encourages parties to economize on disagreement when that would better serve the public.

While partisans legitimately govern with an eye to the next election, they also keep focused on making progress on their agenda, even when they happen to be in the minority. Principled prudence and mutual respect presuppose partisan attitudes and arguments in governing. But they also call on partisan political leaders to seek a better balance between compromising and uncompromising mindsets than is evident in contemporary American politics.

Mixing the Mindsets

The compromising and uncompromising mindsets may be balanced by a division of labor in the institution, with some members consistently accommodating, and others not. This can work only if the intransigent do not always dominate, as often has been the case. A more promising way of achieving a balance is to depend on some members who combine both mindsets. How is this split personality possible? Standing on principle seems to be just the opposite of the disposition needed to advance compromises.

Yet if you are known as a person who stands on principle, specifically on the principles at issue in the negotiations, you are less likely to be seen as compromising too much when you make concessions. Some legislators who are the most successful in leading their colleagues in the land of compromise are also known as among the most strongly committed to certain political principles and ideological programs. Kentucky Senator Henry Clay, known by his admirers as the Great Compromiser for his role in brokering the slavery compromises of the 1820s and 1850, was also a man of strong and consistent principle.[38] His principles were not enlightened by today's standards, but his actions were statesmanlike by the standards of his time. He was a slave owner who believed that the races could never peacefully live together, but he also believed that slavery was holding back national development, and from his earliest days in politics advocated a policy of gradual emancipation. His favored compromise (the so-called omnibus bill) failed at the last minute, and his successful compromises did not last. But the Compromise of 1850 brought ten years of relative peace, and more important, bought time for the North to gain population and industrial strength. As a result, the government that Lincoln eventually led had the resources necessary to save the union.[39]

Although Clay's own principled position was not far from the center of political opinion of his time, holding a centrist position is not a necessary condition for combining the mindsets. In our time the former senator whose comments opened this chapter, Alan Simpson, earned the reputation as a staunch conservative who was also prepared to compromise both to make prog-ress and to prepare the ground for future compromises. Speaking from decades of successful experience in leg-islating, Simpson tells his fellow legislators: "If you can't compromise on anything, go home."[40]

In 1981, Simpson allied with Representative Romano Mazzoli, Democrat from Kentucky, to gain congres-sional passage of immigration reform. What became known as the Simpson-Mazzoli Act took five years of negotiation and debate before Congress approved it in 1986 and President Reagan signed it into law. The bill was a classic compromise, combining conflicting prin-ciples. It criminalized the act of knowingly hiring an illegal immigrant, required employers to attest to their employees' immigration status, created a temporary worker program for agricultural workers (with wage and workplace protections), and also granted amnesty to an estimated three million unauthorized immigrants.[41]

Reaching congressional agreement on this compro-mise took persistence. Congressional opponents had killed so many earlier versions of the bill so many times that they dubbed it "'The Monster from the Blue Lagoon' because of its eerie ability to rise from the dead."[42] Its ability to rise from the dead depended on its support from legislators who combined strong partisan credentials with a compromising mindset. It also benefited from being a carefully crafted agree-ment that employed many strategies to economize on disagreement. That kind of support and those kinds of strategies are likely to be necessary for any successful major immigration reform in this country.

The political careers of Simpson, Kennedy, Hatch, and other legislators with strong partisan credentials testify to both the possibility and the desirability of mixing the mindsets—combining strong partisan principles with recognition that the only way to govern successfully is to compromise on some important issues. They could bring along their colleagues because they had earned their respect for their principled stands in the past. They could drive hard bargains with their adversaries who knew that their positions were principled, and that concessions would be harder for them to make.

Mixing the mindsets in negotiations on a single issue is also often desirable. If you take compromise as your starting point, as some critics complained Obama sometimes did, you may not only put yourself and the principles you believe in at a disadvantage but also reduce the chances of reaching a sustainable compromise. Competing positions typically need to be sharpened and differences clarified before the shape of a final agreement can be seen. We cannot have the "tranquility of resolution without the catharsis of conflict."[43] Timing is of course critical. If the uncompromising mindset continues too long, it feeds on itself and prevents the return of the compromising mindset. Knowing when to shift from one mindset to the other again depends on knowing your colleagues.

The mixing of mindsets can be easily dismissed as flip-flopping or hypocrisy. Yet legislators who effectively mix the mindsets demonstrate a willingness that is often the opposite of those vices. They are willing to sacrifice part of their cause only when it is necessary in order to achieve another part that constitutes a moral gain from their partisan perspective. When their action produces legislative improvements on the status quo, they can honorably defend combining the mindsets.

The ability to put this dual disposition into constructive political action is more likely to be manifest in a political career that spans some time in the same institution with some of the same colleagues. Mixing the mindsets is typically developed and sustained over time in an institution with traditions and customs of collegiality. The Senate in its "golden days" (as they are perhaps too nostalgically remembered) is often cited as the prime example. But any institution that requires members to cooperate on a continuing basis and encourages them to cultivate relationships across oppositional divides can foster this dual disposition. The media and the public play important roles as well. Political leaders can build and enhance their reputations through their career more effectively to the extent that the media and the public find ways of tracking their records of successful compromise.

A Moment of Compromise

Some of the strategies of economizing on disagreement can be seen at work in the polarized 111th Congress, where they helped bring about a rare bipartisan compromise. The compromise took the form of a bill extending tax cuts, unemployment benefits, and other benefits, and was signed into law by President Obama in December 2010.[44] This was the first time he had made a deal with the Republican opposition on major domestic legislation.[45]

The bipartisanship was not the result of a sudden outbreak of holiday cheer. The Democrats had failed to deal with the tax cuts before the November midterm elections. As they surveyed the damage from their shattering electoral defeat, they were in no position to insist on getting their way. For anything to be done before the Republicans took over the House in the next session, the Democrats would have to compromise. Still, some Democrats said they would rather do nothing. They preferred the status quo to the terms of any likely compromise. The Bush-era tax cuts for the wealthy would expire, and the estate tax would return to the higher 2001 levels. But doing nothing would also mean that unemployment benefits would not be extended and middle-class taxes would increase as well.

The political stakes were high, too, as both parties maneuvered to make sure that if taxes increased the other party would be blamed in the next campaign. Political posturing was rife. Senate Republicans announced that they would not vote for cloture on any bills until the matters of federal government funding and tax cuts were concluded, "effectively grab[bing] control of the agenda."[46] Democrats in the House passed a series of what Republican critics called "political-show votes"— actions in favor of legislation that had no chance of success in the Senate but might help their members in the next campaign.[47] A Democratic aide admitted: " 'We may have a vote anyway to get people on the record ... There are a number of leaders who would like a vote even if the Senate is not able to get to 60 votes. It's good for us, it shows we're for the middle class, they are for the rich."[48] The uncompromising mindset was vividly on display in these show votes.

In this contentious climate it was all the more remarkable how often leaders on both sides avoided drawing lines in the sand. Interviewers on the Sunday morning talk shows were regularly frustrated in their attempts to get the leaders to take an unequivocal position on some of the key issues in dispute. Repeatedly pressed on CBS's *Face the Nation*, John Boehner refused to take an absolute stand against a proposal that would cut taxes only for the lower brackets, going so far as to say he would vote for it if that were the only option.[49] His comment did not win favor with many of his colleagues, who promptly issued less accommodating statements. Although Boehner declined to repeat the suggestion that he would vote for such a bill, he never unequivocally declared that he would vote against it.

Democratic leaders had even more trouble with their colleagues who represented the party's base. In the face of a protest by thirty Democratic senators who declared themselves "firmly opposed" to the emerging compromise in mid-December, Harry Reid was remarkably restrained: "This is only a framework. It's up to the Congress to pass it. Some in my caucus still have concerns."[50]

At a press conference in early December in which reporters suggested that the president was compromising his core values and one of them asked, "Where is your line in the sand?" Obama defended not only the proposed compromise but also political compromise in general: "[B]ecause it's a big, diverse country and people have a lot of complicated positions, it means that in order to get stuff done, we're going to compromise... [A]t any given juncture, there are going to be times where my preferred option, what I am absolutely positive is right, I can't get done... [T]he question is, does it make sense for me to tack a little bit this way or tack a little bit that way, because I'm keeping my eye on the long term."[51] While a small group of legislators and White House staff met to try to come up with a compromise, Senate Majority Leader Mitch McConnell and Vice President Joe Biden (each usually accompanied by only a single staff member) began secret meetings.[52] The McConnell-Biden negotiations proved decisive. Because they had worked together for years in the Senate and because they were meeting in private, they were less tempted to indulge in the partisan rhetoric and engage in the personal attacks that often derail such negotiations.

This strategy was not without risk. Influential legislators left out of the discussions might not have been on board for the final push. Some Democrats claimed they had been undercut, especially when it became clear that the final deal would include a generous exemption for wealthy estates.[53] But in return the proposed bill would give Democrats the extension of unemployment benefits and a substantial package of tax breaks for low- and middle-income students, workers, and families with children. The package included a one-year payroll tax cut, which surprised most legislators, because it had not been part of the discussions and was inserted at the last minute. It helped correct what the Democrats saw as an incipient imbalance in the compromise. It also exemplified a variation of the issue separation strategy: bringing a new issue into the negotiations to help conclude a deal.

Many Democrats were still not pleased: "Again and again, we have Democratic presidents who say, 'Don't make the perfect the enemy of the better,' and 'This is the best I can do,'" commented Robert Reich, former labor secretary under President Clinton. "And over and over we have Republican presidents who say, 'I am going to hold out for my principles.'"[54] Yet in this case Obama did hold out for the principle of protecting lower- and middle-income citizens, while giving up on the principle of making the wealthy pay a larger share. Obama had decided he would "test Republicans' willingness to make concessions for economic stimulus measures and 'the Obama tax cuts' for low- and middle-income workers. Then, if Republicans gave him the back of the hand, he would fight."[55] Here his stance was in effect a concurrent merger of the mindsets.

Many Republicans were not enthusiastic about the deal either. They wanted the Bush-era tax cuts made permanent, and they objected to some of the cuts in the Obama package, which in their view would unjustifiably add to the deficit. Indeed, as analysts began to examine the numbers, the balance seemed to favor the Democrats. Of the estimated cost of $900 billion, some $120 billion covered the high-end tax cuts, including the estate tax reduction; $450 billion funded Obama's "wish list"; and $360 billion was for the tax cut extensions both parties favored.[56] That is why one conservative pundit could see the bill as a stealth stimulus, a bigger dose of government spending than Obama's overt stimulus of 2009, and "the biggest stimulus in American history."[57]

The final bill was a classic compromise. Both sides made significant sacrifices. Both had to adjust principles they cared about, but both gained some concessions that promoted other principles they also valued. The leaders on both sides took sharp criticism from those of their base who were still operating in the uncompromising mindset. But beyond the disputes about which party gained or lost more, the compromise served most citizens better than the status quo would have done. Furthermore, it demonstrated a degree of the mutual respect across partisan lines that would be essential for the even more challenging tasks of comprehensive tax reform and deficit reduction, which would require major changes in tax policy and entitlement programs (Social Security, Medicare, and Medicaid). In the polarized politics of our time, the prospects are not bright for any of these reforms, but they are less bleak than they would have been if the tax cut compromise had failed.

The strategies of economizing on disagreement were in evidence throughout the process. Although by no means always in ascendance, a compromising mindset guided the attitudes and actions of enough legislators on both sides to keep the uncompromising mindset in check—at least temporarily. Some legislators were exercising their responsibility to govern, not merely feeding their need to campaign.

But of course electoral calculations were not absent. In a democracy, they never are. In the case of this compromise, which took place in a divided government, electoral calculations may have played a constructive role. Neither party wanted to be blamed for the tax increases that would have occurred if no agreement had been reached, but neither party could be certain who would be blamed more if the compromise failed. When the negative electoral consequences of refusing to compromise are unclear in this way—in effect casting a veil of uncertainty over the coming campaign—the uncompromising mindset normally present in the permanent campaign loses its sting. The least risky course for most legislators then is to try to develop a record of responsible governing, at least on some issues, some of the time.

Compromising in an Uncompromising Time

The even more urgent call to compromise in the summer of 2011—to avoid risking the U.S. government defaulting on its debt—highlights both the possibilities and the perils of compromising in an increasingly uncompromising time.

While the debt ceiling had been raised seventy-eight times since 1960, almost always without serious controversy, the uncompromising mindset was now so pervasive that legislative action seemed doubtful. Private discussions between Vice President Biden and Senate Minority Leader McConnell were critical in breaking the logjam. Their long-term relationship across partisan lines had built the trust that once again proved helpful in reaching agreement. A deal was struck, and the crisis averted.

Yet many thought the deal a sellout.[58] Most who supported the compromise thought it was only better than nothing—not much more to be said for it and a lot more to be said against it. The list of negatives was long: our side gave in far too much to the other; the other side used illegitimate scare tactics; the other side was too cowardly to make the cuts needed to put the country on sound financial footing; and Congress ducked responsibility for solving any of the big financial problems facing the country. In sum, the deal did little more than "kick the can down the road."[59]

What happened after the can was kicked down the road provides a key lesson for compromising in an uncompromising time: there is no substitute for the willingness of enough partisan legislators to mix their mindsets. As if to acknowledge the paltry benefits of its provisions, the August bill tried to compel a bigger and better compromise just a few months later by delegating the power to make the next compromise to a "supercommittee"—the Joint Select Committee on Deficit Reduction—consisting of only twelve members, six from each chamber. The supercommittee was charged with coming up with a plan by November 23 to reduce federal budget deficits by a total of at least $1.5 trillion over ten years. Its recommendations would become law if voted by a simple majority of both congressional houses—significantly, without any filibuster, amendments, or other procedural blocks permitted. If a majority of the committee failed to agree, the government would automatically have to cut spending across the board in hundreds of military and nonmilitary programs, including Medicare. The package of these so-called trigger cuts was unpalatable to both parties, and it was supposed to provide a strong incentive to reach agreement on a better compromise. The threat was not as immediate as a governmental default or shutdown, and some members may have thought that even if the trigger were pulled, there would still be time to avoid the cuts.

The supercommittee failed to use its super powers. Although it had almost unprecedented legislative authority, it squandered the rare opportunity to produce a grand compromise like that proposed by the bipartisan Bowles-Simpson Commission in 2010. The supercommittee could not reach any deal at all, although a sizable majority of Americans said that they wanted a compromise even if it meant sacrificing some of their favored positions. Its failure showed that even suspending the long-standing institutional procedures that often block compromise will not suffice unless enough legislators are willing to mix their mindsets. Under the supercommittee's rules, it would have been enough if just one partisan had been willing to break ranks with the uncompromising party line.

When the uncompromising mindset takes over governing despite an impending crisis, it imperils even its own usefulness in campaigning. Public approval ratings of both parties in Congress hit historic lows. Yet having collectively taken compromise off the table, legislators left themselves no alternative but to wait for the next election, when they would hope to convince enough voters that they and their party should have the opportunity to govern without compromising.[60] This may be the hope of every legislator with an uncompromising mindset, but it is not a strategy for responsible governance. Nor is it what most citizens have signaled that they want.

It is unlikely that one party will gain complete control in the next election (securing the reliable sixty votes needed to overcome a filibuster in the Senate). And even if one party were to gain control, it would still face the daunting task of making compromises within its own ranks. Whatever the outcome in 2012, the American people were ill-served in this shameful process in 2011. And as long as politicians believe that adopting only the uncompromising mindset is the best way to win the next election, the campaign will continue, and governing will wither.

Even at these moments when the need for a willingness to take responsibility for governing is greatest, the compulsion to continue campaigning persists. As the next chapter shows, the tension between campaigning and governing may be as permanent as contemporary campaigns themselves have become. But as the final chapter suggests, that tension is compatible with creating more space for the compromising mindset to govern responsibly.

4

CAMPAIGNING V. GOVERNING

Even politicians who appreciate compromise campaign with an uncompromising mindset. They must know that this stance will stiffen the opposition and prime their supporters to resist compromise when the time comes to govern. They also know that to govern effectively in a pluralist society they will have to make some difficult compromises. Why, then, don't they anticipate the compromise problem in their campaigns and educate voters about the need for accommodation?

Consider two politicians running for president. Call one Obama the Tenacious and the other Obama the Cooperative. The first declares that one of his priorities is to reform health care. Among other bold initiatives, he promises a "National Health Insurance Exchange to help increase competition by insurers," which would include a public option. He states his unequivocal opposition to any law that requires everyone to buy health insurance (the individual mandate), an approach favored by his main rival in the primary. He promises that his proposal for health-care reform "won't add a dime to the deficit and is paid for up front." Although he presents himself as willing to "reach across the aisle," he mentions no possible concessions during the campaign and insists he will press forward with or without support from the opposition party.[1]

This portrait is a recognizable likeness of the actual Barack Obama in the campaigns leading up to the election in 2008. Now imagine a more compromise-inclined Obama. Instead of standing firmly in favor of a public option, Obama the Cooperative decides to educate the public about the need for compromise. While expressing his own positions, he also states explicitly where he is willing to make concessions and outlines the deals he is prepared to accept. He announces that he is willing to compromise with the opponents of a public option by substituting voluntary state experiments. He also anticipates one of the compromises that was in fact offered later to try to resolve the abortion controversy. He announces that, if necessary to pass health-care reform, he would be willing to give states permission to bar the use of federal subsidies for insurance plans that cover abortion (and require all insurers in states that do not adopt this ban to divide their subsidy money into separate accounts so that only dollars from private premiums can be used to pay for abortions).

In private, the actual Obama reportedly indicated that, once in office, he would be inclined to compromise on health care. Alluding to the Clintons' failed effort at reform, he said he would not "develop his own plan, drop it on the Capitol steps like a 'stone tablet,' and refuse to bargain." He remarked, "If Daniel Patrick Moynihan or Bill Bradley or John Chaffee came to me with the possibility of compromising I'm not going to tell them, 'It's my way or the highway.' "[2] But this accommodating attitude was not the public stance that Obama took. During the campaign, he stood more like Obama the Tenacious.

No candidate is likely to campaign as Obama the Cooperative does because campaigning is not conducive to the compromising mindset. Nor is it the appropriate realm to announce concessions a politician ultimately may be willing to make to strike a good legislative deal. Campaigning is an activity that by its nature places certain constraints on candidates. The constraints limit the extent to which a candidate can champion compromise, but they cannot themselves be considered a democratic deformity that should be corrected. They are not pathologies but requisites of a healthy democratic process. The uncompromising mindset serves these requisites of campaigning.

Requisites of Campaigning

"I actually did vote for the $87 billion [to support the Iraq war] before I voted against it."[3] With these fateful words in the 2004 campaign, John Kerry opened himself to one of the most dreaded charges in a political campaign—flip-flopping. The Bush campaign quickly took advantage of his comment, repeating it in ads that concluded with the question, "How can John Kerry protect us ... when he doesn't even know where he stands?"[4] Although the ad was misleading, its message stuck because in a campaign the suspicion of inconsistency is ever-present. The test of knowing where you stand seems to be just that you keep standing in the same place. Democratic strategists too say they are "ready to pounce on any candidate who switches positions in the hunt for the nomination as lacking core convictions." In 2011, they indicated that they were "particularly keen on doing so against Mr. Romney, who [was] still facing such accusations from his 2008 campaign."[5]

Tenaciously standing on principle, as the uncompromising mindset demands, not only provides protection against charges of inconsistency; it also satisfies other needs of campaigning. Most important is political mobilization. Candidates are less effective in inspiring supporters when they talk more about prudent compromises than about steadfast commitments. Their support and ultimately their success in the campaign depend on reaffirming their uncompromising commitment to core principles and on distinguishing their positions sharply from those of their opponents.[6] Voters need to see the differences between the candidates as clearly as possible. In candidate-centered campaigns that have become more prevalent in our time, the differences that matter are to be found less in the issues than in the personalities.[7] Here an uncompromising image may itself be an advantage, even if what the candidate is unwilling to compromise on remains vague.

The Republican campaign strategy in 2002 and 2004, alternately credited to or blamed on Bush's political adviser Karl Rove, was as sharp a repudiation of the compromising mindset as has been seen in recent years. The aim was to target the base and mostly ignore the middle. Its success spawned many imitators, and for a while seemed to usher in an era of strategic polarization. But, as political scientists point out, the strategy works in general elections only under special conditions—only if the base is bigger than that of the other party and also near a majority in size.[8] Campaigning does not require appealing only to the base, but it does require directing attention to your most likely supporters, usually those already inclined toward you or your party.

"Targeting" is the "foundation of virtually every aspect of campaign strategy."[9] Unlike a legislator who might try to reach across the aisle to recruit cosponsors for a bill by inviting amendments, candidates do not benefit from trying to persuade the opposition by making concessions. A candidate has little or nothing to gain by making concessions. The overriding aim is to mobilize supporters, not to persuade opponents.[10]

Although political scientists no longer insist that campaigns have only "minimal effects" (as the conventional wisdom in the field long held), they continue to find that most campaigns largely reinforce attitudes that most voters had before the campaign started.[11] Most voters cast their ballots on the basis of "fundamentals": the performance of the economy, partisan identification, and ideological compatibility.[12] Most voters do not change their views about these fundamentals during a campaign. Even most of the undecided and independent voters eventually follow their pre-campaign partisan inclinations.

Campaigns are nonetheless important. Although they do not change basic attitudes and beliefs, they can bring voters' choices into line with their preexisting attitudes and beliefs about the fundamentals, and they can mobilize groups to go to the polls. This is why campaigns matter, and it is also why campaigning does not welcome compromising.

Another requisite of campaigning supported by standing on principle is anticipatory bargaining. This is the need to stay alert to the effects that your campaign strategy may have later on your legislative leverage. Signaling a willingness to compromise on specific policies before your opponents offer anything in return is obviously not a strategy designed to achieve the most you can reasonably win in the legislative negotiations to come. Avoiding such signals is not only a strategic imperative but also a moral requirement. Candidates have a responsibility to their followers to increase the chances of achieving what they stand for. Furthermore, the process of compromise itself, properly conceived, involves mutual sacrifice, which expresses a reciprocity that is absent when candidates make premature concessions. Even if Ronald Reagan had known that he would have to accept higher corporate rates to get the tax reform he wanted, he would have been not only politically foolish but also morally irresponsible to say so in the campaign.

Campaigning also requires mutual mistrust, the second element of the uncompromising mindset. Campaigns are competitive encounters, not cooperative enterprises. They are contests with zero-sum outcomes, not opportunities for win-win solutions. Candidates aim to outmaneuver and defeat their opponents; they inevitably operate in an environment rife with suspicion and manipulation. Mutual mistrust is not only understandable but advisable. Even on the rare occasions when candidates are forced to negotiate compromises— when they have to agree on the schedule and format of televised debates, for example—their managers try to arrange terms that will advantage their respective candidates, not necessarily those that could serve a common interest in informing the voters.

Because a robust campaign requires candidates to treat their opponents as adversaries who must be defeated rather than colleagues who should be worked with, we should not be surprised that so much campaign advertising is negative. Nor should we be so quick to condemn it. Negative attack ads may not be more effective than positive advertising.[13] Nor is there evidence that they increase cynicism and reduce turn-out.[14] But there is evidence that negative ads are more informative than positive ones.[15] By their nature, the negative ads have to be more specific and offer more evidence. Rather than corrupting the campaign, some negative advertising may actually improve it. Of course, false and misleading negative ads should be condemned. An uncompromising mindset does not countenance deception or unfairness, and a vigorous campaign does not need it. But in a respectably conducted campaign, attacks that would be out of place in the halls of a legislature can play a constructive role.

In any campaign, the incentives for mutual respect are limited. There are plenty of reasons to mistrust your opponents, and few to demonstrate respect for them. If candidates respect one another, it is usually only the kind of respect that a gladiator has for the skills of a formidable combatant. Even in primary campaigns in which candidates share the same values and hold similar positions on the issues, we do not see an abundance of mutual respect.

Candidates may begin with good will toward each other, telling themselves not to take the criticisms personally. But they often end up expressing (usually privately) feelings of disdain and bitterness, which tend to persist long after the contest is over. This animosity hangover from the campaign is not helpful in establishing the relationships that candidates later need to govern effectively. Campaigns are not designed to cultivate continuing relationships among candidates. They would serve their competitive function less well if they were.

Two Conceptions of Democracy

This picture of campaigning does not fit well with the classic ideal of a citizen that some democratic theorists favor—an open-minded individual listening to all sides, carefully considering the issues, and coming to a well-informed conclusion. It might seem especially unfriendly toward a deliberative conception of democracy. Deliberative democrats advocate vigorous debate—which campaigning favors. But they also ask politicians to stand ready to acknowledge error, modify their positions as new evidence and better arguments come to light, and accommodate opponents' views as far as possible to make political progress—all of which campaigning shuns.

Yet deliberative democrats do not believe that deliberation should happen all—or even most—of the time. They can recognize that campaigns are not a promising environment for deliberation. It would be not only unrealistic but also undesirable to try to convert campaigns into prime sites for deliberation. That would undermine the strategically competitive character of campaigning. To the extent that the candidates who would be best at governing decide to try to campaign by being best at deliberating, they would quickly become the worst at winning. They would lose the opportunity to govern. The best would become the worst.

Deliberative democrats can still consistently argue that the quality of campaign discussion should be improved, and that debates should provide opportunities for constructive dialogue. But they too must recognize that campaigns by their nature are strategic and competitive interactions, not deliberative exchanges. Campaigns do not serve their function if opponents are cooperating when they should be competing. Reason-giving in such circumstances tends to be exclusively strategic. It provides a poor model for the more robust deliberation that should take place before and after a campaign. The habits of deliberation need to be cultivated elsewhere.[16]

Does this account of campaigning then favor a competitive conception of democracy? Joseph Schumpeter, the seminal proponent of the competitive conception, defined democracy as "that institutional arrangement for arriving at political decisions in which individuals acquire the power to decide by means of a competitive struggle for the people's vote."[17] The requisites of campaigning constitute a competitive process that could well be regarded as a struggle. But Schumpeter developed this idea of competition in a highly elitist direction, which is neither necessary nor desirable in contemporary politics.[18]

Democracy is diminished in two ways when it is reduced to a competition for power among elites. First, after citizens elect a leader, they "must refrain from instructing him about what he is to do."[19] The "no backseat driving rule" is intended to leave elites free to govern without the pressures of campaigning.[20] This leads to a more rigid division between campaigning and governing than a robust democracy should permit. Even while governing, politicians have to try to build support for their policies and respond to criticisms of their policies. As we have argued, campaigning and its uncompromising mindset should play a role in governing, but the role should be in deference to—not in domination of—the goals of governing.

A second elitist feature in Schumpeter's conception also dilutes democracy. His view of electoral competition does not exclude "cases that are strikingly analogous to the economic phenomena we label 'unfair' or 'fraudulent' competition or restraint of competition."[21] This is "as it should be," Schumpeter argued, "if we wish to understand and not to philosophize."[22] This kind of understanding provides little or no basis for reforms that are intended to reduce corruption and unfair influence in campaigns.

Some contemporary defenders of a competitive theory do philosophize, and some have developed a competitive theory that is less elitist. For example, political theorist Ian Shapiro defends a competitive conception but revises Schumpeter in several ways to encourage more competition both during and between elections.[23] Rather than reducing democracy to competition, theorists like Shapiro view competition for power as one indispensable part of any desirable democracy.[24] With this, deliberative democrats would agree. Also like deliberative democrats, these competitive theorists trust that citizens are competent to express their views about issues and play a part in governing, not only in elections. They want elections to be a competition for power and also to uphold a robust democratic right to political equality. They also argue in favor of campaign finance reform to constrain the power of money in politics.[25]

But competitive theorists are critical of compromise between political partisans, viewing it as a form of duopolistic power: "If competition for power is the lifeblood of democracy, then the search for bipartisan consensus (along with the ideal of deliberative agreement that lies behind it) is really anticompetitive collusion in restraint of democracy."[26] This blanket critique of bipartisan compromise turns competition into the first and dominant principle of democracy (constrained only by judicial protection of rights). If that were all there were to democracy, citizens would not be as frustrated as they have been in recent years by the inability of partisans to govern in the face of economic crises. As democratic citizens regularly remind their leaders, bipartisan compromise—not necessarily consensus—is often necessary to govern effectively.

Competitive theorists advocate using antitrust laws and ballot initiatives to break up what they regard as the anticompetitive power of the two parties. "Why is it that people do not challenge legislation that has bipartisan backing, or other forms of bipartisan agreement, on *these* grounds?"[27] These theorists do not appear to recognize that any such challenge would require deliberation, along with political mobilization and success in competitive elections, to convince citizens that they would be well served by breaking the duopoly of the two major parties. Such reforms would not avoid the need for compromise. In any case, if a movement to end two-party dominance ever succeeded, new parties would enter the political fray. Then there would be an even greater need to compromise in order to avoid political gridlock and to pass legislation for any progress to be made.

The only alternative to compromise between parties at the national level is the equivalent of monopolistic governing power by one party for an extended period of time, which would mean combining control of the executive with supermajorities in Congress. That alternative hardly seems a desirable long-term solution, even if it were probable. In the meantime, bipartisan or multipartisan compromise will be both necessary and desirable for good governance, whether or not one subscribes to a deliberative theory of democracy.

Compromise draws on an appreciation of both competition and deliberation in democracy. Although we argue that campaigning has intruded too much into governing, we would also object to trying to banish the campaigning mindset entirely from governing. The problem is that campaigning and its uncompromising mindset have come to have an overwhelming role in governing in the United States—and increasingly in other democracies as well. This state of affairs should find favor with no conception of democracy. All presuppose that when campaigning ends, the winning candidates should lead and govern well rather than simply continue to campaign for the next election. Democracy is not deliberation or competition through and through.

Neither a deliberative nor a competitive conception of democracy can be a complete guide to the role of compromise if its core ideal is taken to rule all parts of the democratic process. The competitive ideal has to be restrained in governing in order to reach compromises, and the deliberative ideal has to be tempered in campaigning in order to provide choices. Yet neither would it be desirable simply to limit each conception to what might be thought to be its own sphere—a competitive conception for campaigning and a deliberative conception for governing. Both competition and deliberation have a place throughout the democratic process. Any adequate conception of democracy should make room for both ideals.

That still leaves open the question: with what conception should we determine the balance between the ideals—when and to what degree one should prevail?

We have argued elsewhere that the deliberative conception, properly understood, provides the basis for assessing democratic practices, including nondeliberative ones.[28] It does not prescribe deliberative practices in all or even most parts of the democratic process. But it does require that all practices be justified deliberatively at some point, and that they remain open to deliberative challenge at any point. Deliberative democracy requires mutual reason-giving. Citizens and their representatives are expected to justify to one another the laws they adopt and the lawmaking practices by which they adopt them. The mutual justifications are to take the form of reasons that could be accepted by free and equal persons seeking fair terms of cooperation. The reasons should be given in a public forum, and the participants should be prepared to change their minds when they hear good reasons for doing so.

What does a deliberative assessment of the relative roles of campaigning and governing require? We have already indicated how a deliberative assessment of campaigning would proceed. It would acknowledge that competitive campaigns are a desirable and probably the best feasible practice for enabling free and equal citizens to choose their representatives. It would also recognize that an uncompromising mindset is necessary to sustain this competitive practice. But the form of competitive practices must be justified to and by citizens, which means that deliberation ultimately determines the limits of competition. An aim of such limits would be to keep the competition appropriate in campaigning from overwhelming the deliberation necessary for governing.

As for governing, we showed in the previous chapter how the compromising mindset is needed to produce legislation that improves over the status quo. But an assessment of the place of campaigning in governing is more complex, because governing itself is complex; it serves many different and sometimes conflicting goals. Consider just two of the most important: good legislation and responsive legislators—or more generally, justice and accountability. To produce good legislation, legislators have to be able to use their discretion and judgment to negotiate compromises that improve on the status quo, but they also have to be responsive to their constituents as a matter not only of political survival but also of democratic duty.

The duty of accountability means that anticipating the next campaign (and respecting the last) should not be excluded from the practice of governing. Exactly how much anticipation (and respect) is desirable cannot be specified by a general rule or principle. But although the optimal amount of campaigning in governing cannot be precisely determined, the upper limit is clear enough. It is reached at the point at which campaigning dominates governing. At the extreme, legislators have nothing to be accountable for—except for doing nothing but campaigning for reelection.

So we can say: to the extent that campaigning with its uncompromising mindset dominates governing between elections, it is less acceptable. It dominates governing if its attitudes and activities continue at nearly the same level or in the same form as during the campaign itself. The system is out of balance if legislators have no respite from the pressures of campaigning between elections. When campaigning has no discernible boundaries in space or time, it does not serve the democratic process well. Campaigning has gone too far when it goes on continuously. That is what we now see in this era of the permanent campaign.[29]

Campaigns without End

A successful campaign strategy requires the opposite of a compromising mindset. It favors candidates who stand firmly on their principles and condemn their opponents' positions at every turn. Candidates sometimes modify their positions to reach independents in general elections, but they do so less than is usually assumed, and even that gesture toward the center is often suspect in the eyes of their more ardent supporters. The primary election, which typically permits only party members to participate, effectively requires candidates to maximize their uncompromising stands to capture their partisan base, which along with the media will assail primary winners if they diverge from their hard lines in the general election.

But to govern, elected leaders who want to get anything done have to adopt a compromising mindset. Rather than standing tenaciously on principle, they need to make concessions. Rather than mistrusting and trying to defeat their opponents at every turn, they have to respect their opponents enough to collaborate on legislation. In their acceptance speeches, many elected officials signal their intention to move to a compromising mindset by vowing to be everyone's president—or governor, senator, or representative—and declaring now to be the time for coming together. They may begin by governing, but they soon revert to campaigning.

The permanent campaign does not leave much space for the compromising mindset. The division of labor between campaigning and governing, once passably clear, has dissolved.[30] Political leaders increasingly rely on political consultants, pollsters, and focus groups to formulate public policy. Interest groups and their lobbyists constantly remind politicians that what they do in office will affect whether they stay in office—reminders that often come as offers not to be refused. Politicians spend more and more time between elections raising funds for their next campaigns. Journalists increasingly cover governing as if it were campaigning.

The grueling nature of campaigns themselves—the personal attacks, the pressures to raise huge sums for oneself and the party, the never-ending travel—makes elective office less attractive to candidates who want to legislate and who might be inclined to collaborate and compromise. Recruiting and retaining the natural governors, politicians who know how to compromise when necessary, becomes more difficult. The field is increasingly left to insurgents, ideologues, and the hyperambitious.

Not all the consequences of the permanent campaign are undesirable. It has probably helped create a process that is more inclusive and more transparent than before. It has also made the process more responsive—though arguably more to special interests than to citizens generally. But its effect on the capacity for compromise and on time spent on governing is largely negative.

The more that campaigning comes to dominate governing in democratic politics, the harder compromise becomes.[31] During an exchange with congressional Republicans just ten days after the Massachusetts election that gave the GOP a Senate seat critical to their filibuster power, President Obama observed: "It's very hard to have the kind of bipartisan work" we need on health care and other problems if the "whole question is structured as a talking point for running a campaign."[32] As the mindset useful for campaigning overtakes the mindset needed for governing, leaders—wherever they stand on the political spectrum—are less likely to see, let alone seize, opportunities for desirable compromise. Although the dominance of the uncompromising over the compromising mindset is not necessarily equal in all parties or across all factions within a party, the pressures of the permanent campaign exempt no party and few politicians from its powerful incentives to deadlock more and compromise less.

Even when elected leaders do recognize the desirability of compromise, their staunchest supporters still want to hold them to their campaign promises and believe that the leaders are exaggerating the need for concessions. The expectations raised by the previous campaign continue to hang over the business of governing. Campaign promises stated in absolute terms limit the flexibility of legislators, even those who do not care about reelection.

That is precisely the purpose of the pledges that advocacy groups seek from candidates, a practice that escalated in the presidential campaign in 2011, "the year of the pledge."[33] The pledges included commitments to the Americans for Tax Reform declaration never to raise taxes for any reason, the Susan B. Anthony List promise, in which candidates vow to cut off funding for abortion, and the Marriage Vow in which candidates agree to oppose same sex marriage, reject Sharia law, and swear to be faithful to their spouse. Rick Santorum, a Republican presidential candidate and former senator from Pennsylvania, wrote that "signing a pledge is a good way to strengthen our political promises." As one political scientist observed, it is also a way for voters who believe that "compromise is invalid…it's selling out your principles" to send a message: "hold the line, we don't want you to compromise."[34]

The effects of these pledges on governing are especially insidious because the politicians who make them believe they are acting on principle, and they have convinced themselves that they cannot make concessions without violating their personal integrity. Yet in signing these pledges they have signed away their responsibility to govern. The terms of complex legislative compromises necessary for governing typically cannot be predicted in advance of negotiations. The most successful compromises, like the Tax Reform Act, often require the parties to modify their views about what is acceptable in the process of crafting the compromise. No one could have predicted the final shape of the tax or health-care reform bills, and few could have predicted some of the issues that would become major sticking points. Absolute promises may be good for campaigns and marriages, but they are bad for good government.

As soon as one campaign ends, the preparations for the next one begin. Positions become even more rigid, and differences sharpen even further, as both sides look toward the next election. Individual egos play a role, too. Politicians who want credit for passing legislation (or for stopping it) refuse to cooperate with their allies (or try to undermine their opponents) when they do not get their way. The minority party adopts as its main goal the regaining of power in the next election and sees obstruction as its principal means for achieving

it. As minority leader, Mitch McConnell candidly described his strategy: "The single most important thing
we want to achieve is for President Obama to be a one-
term president."[35] If this kind of strategy proves successful, it is likely to provoke similar obstruction from
the other party when it finds itself in the minority. In
the cycle of obstruction that ensues, no party is able to
govern well. The last campaign no less than the next
can thwart compromise, as they merge to create one
continuous activity that overtakes governing.

The problems of the permanent campaign are most
pronounced in the United States, where the period of
campaigning is unlimited and the term-lengths of many
offices are shorter.[36] But they are not entirely absent in
any democracy in which the habits of the campaign
persist in the routines of government. Several studies
of the "Americanization" of campaigns in Europe and
other developed democracies have found more than a
few signs of the spread of the permanent campaign. Although the character of campaigns varies according to
local customs and political culture, nearly all are looking more and more like those in the United States.[37]
As this trend continues, many other democracies are
likely to confront the challenge of keeping campaigning in its place.

No one should suppose that we could return to a
time when governing and campaigning stayed more
reliably in separate spheres, each minding its own
business. The process then was in many respects less

democratic, and no more edifying than in our time. But
to improve the prospects of compromising today, we
need to find ways to keep the pressures of campaigning
from taking over the business of governing. This task
is challenging, because many causes of the rise of the
permanent campaign are themselves permanent. Consider just this short list, compiled by political scientist Hugh Heclo: the rise of candidate-centered politics,
the polarization of the parties, the expansion of interest group politics, the growth of new communication
technologies, the pervasiveness of political consultants
and pollsters, the swelling appetite for political money,
and the higher stakes in a system in which government
is more extensive and more active.[38] And this list does
not include structural constraints that exacerbate the
problem, such as short terms mandated by the Constitution or legal restrictions like the prohibition of open
primaries. In the next chapter we consider ways in
which governing might be combined with campaigning
without all the mischiefs of the permanent campaign.

5

GOVERNING WITH CAMPAIGNING

In face of the permanent pressures sustaining the permanent campaign, we should not expect to find any reforms that could completely insulate governing from campaigning. Nor should we want such a sharp separation between the two. In a democracy, politicians care about reelection while they are governing, not only while they are campaigning. Also, to win support for their legislative proposals, they often need to use many of the tools of campaigning (direct appeals to voters, town meetings, barnstorming, and the like). In a divided government, going directly to the voters may be the only way to break a legislative stalemate. When legislators are intransigent, leaders can turn to the voters. They can campaign for compromise.

While governing does not preclude campaigning, it does require some room to operate. As we saw in the previous chapter, the permanent campaign does not give governing much leeway. We should try to find some reforms that could protect the capacity to govern, making democracy safer for governing, without completely suppressing the impulse to campaign while in office. Although campaigning cannot be banished from governing, its influence can be restrained. In this chapter, we suggest ways that several practices in government, elections, and the media might be modified to make more scope for governing.

Space for Governing

In January 2011, Mark Udall, Democratic senator from Colorado, proposed that each member of Congress sit with a colleague from the other party at the State of the Union Address. He lamented "the departure from statesmanship and collegiality [that] is fueled, in part, by contentious campaigns and divisive rhetoric," and reinforced by "the choreographed standing and clapping of one side of the room—while the other side sits." He urged the new sitting arrangement to demonstrate that members of Congress "can debate our differences with respect, honor and civility." Fifty-nine members signed his petition calling for initiating this "small but important new tradition in American politics."[1] Some 150 members ultimately paired off with colleagues from the other party. No one expected what some members called "date night" to result in a sudden resurgence of bipartisan cooperation. And of course it did not. But as a symbolic act, which was what Udall intended, it succeeded in dramatizing the message that in a legislature individual interactions are necessary for collective achievements. Proximity facilitates collegiality: legislators who sit together work together better. Institutional geography matters.

The implications of this message can be extended to more consequential proposals. When Newt Gingrich became Speaker in 1995, he told freshman Republicans that they should not move their families to Washington. He wanted them to spend more time campaigning in their districts. As Representative Jim Cooper remembers, "Soon everyone belonged to the Tuesday–Thursday Club. Members became strangers, the easier for them to fight."[2] The pattern persists today in even more exaggerated form. Elected legislators associate with like-minded members during their fleeting time in Washington and with like-minded constituents when they return to their districts. Congressional life has come to mirror the partitioned conditions that social scientists find lead to polarized and often extreme views.[3]

To encourage more sustained interaction, veteran congressional observer Norm Ornstein proposes that Congress change its schedule—three weeks on, one week off. During the three-week period, Congress would be in session from nine to five, Monday through Friday. "This would create opportunity for debate and deliberation, and provide a powerful incentive for members to move their families to Washington."

Ornstein would have the government provide a housing allowance, along with at-cost rental apartments in two newly constructed buildings near the Capitol. The apartments would include "childcare facilities and a common eating space to make them family friendly and to encourage socializing."[4] Members living closer together might not find common legislative ground, but they would be more likely to better understand their disagreements and moderate the mistrust that blocks consideration of compromise.

When adversaries know each other well, they are far more likely to recognize whether the other side's refusal to compromise on a principle is a negotiating tactic or a real political constraint. They are less likely to act as players in the classic bargaining game who hold out for their maximum individual payoff, producing an outcome that makes both sides worse off. In longer-term relationships, legislators have a better sense of their colleagues' intentions, their trustworthiness, and the political constraints they are facing—and their colleagues know that they do. They are repeat players. That enables all to make more confident judgments about when to compromise and when not to.

Another recommendation would create some safe harbors for bipartisanship by partitioning parts of the legislative process—subjecting some to procedural rules that are more conducive to cooperation. Representative David Price, a Democrat from North Carolina and one of the few political scientists in Congress, urges movement in the direction of the "restrained partisanship that has historically characterized committee operations."[5] He points out that legislators of both parties share the responsibility for holding the executive branch accountable—the constitutional power of the purse. That institutional role "should be distinct from jockeying for partisan advantage within Congress." Campaigning tactics on the floor of the House could remain the same on many other issues, but for appropriations Price recommends tightening procedures (such as the open rule, which permits an indefinite number of amendments without any effective limit on the time for debate) in order to restore a more accommodating mode on the floor as well as in committee.

To the extent that one part of the process operates less in the campaign mode, it puts the compromising mindset on display. A good example, on occasion, not only could produce better results but also could serve as a model for conduct in other parts of the legislative process. For similar reasons, congressional investigations, ethics proceedings, and criminal referrals should be more effectively protected from blatantly partisan attempts to use them to stockpile political fodder for the next campaign. Letting the independent counsel statute expire in 1999 was a step in the right direction, enabling the process of special investigations to be more publicly accountable through the Justice Depart-ment.[6] Nothing can entirely substitute, however, for some modicum of self-restraint on the part of partisan public officials.

Democratic theorists as well as democratic citi-zens recognize that it is important to preserve ample space for opposition in government.[7] A robust opposi-tion serves to keep the ruling party honest, provides an outlet for dissent, and helps a current minority to accept laws they otherwise oppose. The government endures and parties cooperate in part because the ma-jority knows that it could find itself in the minority in the future. In the United States Senate, however, this logic has been carried to an extreme. Supermajority rules and customs, notably the filibuster, protect the minority so well that the majority will is often com-pletely thwarted.[8] Nearly all legislation and most con-firmations in effect now require sixty votes. The use of the filibuster has grown steadily and dramatically— from affecting about 8 percent of major measures annu-ally in the 1960s to 70 percent in recent years.[9] At the same time, the use of still more problematic tactics of obstruction, such as the holds that individual senators place on nominations, has sharply increased.

To be sure, the filibuster can sometimes promote compromise. When a legislative body with a superma-jority rule is as closely divided as the Senate has been in recent years, then the majority party must make concessions in order to win the votes of at least some members of the minority party. Indeed, the threat of filibuster can even force a compromise on the procedure itself, as happened in the case of President Bush's nomination of Samuel Alito to the Supreme Court in 2005.[10] The Democrats, then in the minority, declared their intention to filibuster the nomination. In response, the Republicans threatened to change the Senate rules to allow a simple majority to ban judicial filibusters. They called the move the "constitutional option." Others called it the "nuclear option" because the Democrats said that they would retaliate by shutting down the Senate completely. Neither party really wanted procedural warfare to go this far. One reason was the veil of uncertainty about the effect on public opinion: neither party was sure who would be blamed for the collapse of legislative business.[11]

A group of seven Democrats and seven Republicans in the Senate—"the Gang of Fourteen"—reached a compromise that brought temporary peace. They agreed for the rest of the 109th Congress to oppose any change in the cloture rule, to let three of the ten contested judicial nominees receive confirmation votes, and to limit any filibuster of judicial nominees to "extraordinary circumstances." Neither side was pleased with the outcome. Political scientists are still debating which side gained or lost more.[12] But the compromise averted a collapse of the legislative process, which, whatever its effect on the parties' campaign strategies, would not have served the cause of good government.

The way the filibuster has evolved shows that supermajority rules—far from being necessary or sufficient for compromise—routinely thwart it. It may be
true that under such rules the parties must compromise
if any action is to be taken. But notice the "if." The
alternative—no action—is more likely. When no action
is taken, the resulting political stalemate blocks improvements over the status quo just as surely as if the
uncompromising mindset had prevailed without any
threat of a filibuster. Moreover, as Congress has become
more polarized, the filibuster has become a tool used
more by the minority party than by other minorities.[13]
The content of the compromises achieved in this way
tends to produce results that are more useful in mobilizing the base in the next campaign than in satisfying
the interests of the general electorate.[14] The "filibuster
pivot"—the senator whose vote is needed to meet the
supermajority threshold—"will generally be a minority party member who is relatively far from the floor
median and especially distant from the majority party
median."[15]

Yet the filibuster is likely to survive—either because
majorities will not be able to abolish it or because both
majority and minority parties find it in their interest to
keep it.[16] But it is not obviously in the public's interest.
As Tocqueville warned, "a minority of the nation domi-
nating the Senate could completely paralyze the will of
the majority... and that is contrary to the spirit of constitutional government."[17] The filibuster may well make

more space for the minority, but whether it encourages the kind of compromise that protects governing from campaigning or whether it produces any compromises at all depends on factors beyond the rules themselves. Rather than celebrating the filibuster's preservation, we need to look for ways of increasing the chances that it will be used for compromises more attuned to governing rather than campaigning. The chances will be greater to the extent that the compromising mindset is more generally encouraged in the legislature.

We have concentrated on making space for governing in the legislative branch, where campaigning is very much on members' minds. But presidents and their advisers think about the next election too—and how much they do so partly depends on the institutional locus of their thinking. President Jimmy Carter established what would become the Office of Political Affairs in the White House (OPA), which has "come to represent the centralization of electoral politics in the White House."[18] Its influence on governing reached a peak in the second term of the Bush administration. According to an investigation by the Office of Special Counsel, the OPA's activities led to numerous violations of the Hatch Act, which prohibits most federal employees from engaging in partisan political activity.[19] For example, the OPA organized some seventy-five political briefings for agency officials, which were intended (as described by one advocate) to "keep the troops informed, motivated and activated as we move forward toward the fall elections."[20] Among its several recommendations that could help keep campaigning at bay, the Special Counsel report urged Congress to abolish the OPA. Obama closed the OPA when he moved his campaign operation to Chicago to prepare for the 2012 election, but Congress has left the door open for future presidents to resurrect the political operation in the White House.

A former associate counsel to President George W. Bush, reflecting on his experience when Karl Rove headed the Office of Political Affairs, would go further. He favors rules that would prohibit all White House staff members from "engaging in personal capacity political activity" and would ban "any political activity on government property, whether in the White House or anywhere else."[21] His proposal would prevent the political parties from organizing events such as the meeting sponsored by the Democratic National Committee in March 2011 at which thirty business leaders, all former or potential contributors, discussed the economy with the president, staff, and DNC officials.[22]

To pursue these and other efforts at protecting the space for governing would be to carry on the struggle begun as early as the presidency of Thomas Jefferson. As one of his first acts in office, he requested that the heads of executive departments order employees "not [to] attempt to influence the votes of others nor take any part in the business of electioneering, that being deemed inconsistent with the spirit of the Constitution and [the employees'] duties to it."[23]

Term Time

If protecting space for governing is important, so is making time for it. One period of time that matters greatly to legislators is the length of their service. It might therefore be thought that term limits would be a useful device to concentrate the minds of legislators on governing. If they did not need to spend time preparing for their next campaign, they would not have to worry about agreeing to compromises that might be unpopular with their constituents. They would not be preoccupied with fundraising. They could get on with the business of making laws.

The controversy about term limits has a long life, beginning with Aristotle's claim that democracy requires "all to rule and be ruled in turn."[24] Contemporary proponents argue that "elected officials who remain in office too long become preoccupied with reelection and ignore their duties as representatives of the people." Such "entrenched incumbency" reduces voter participation and "has led to an electoral system that is less free, less competitive, and less representative" than it should be.[25] Opponents argue that term limits reduce choice by eliminating candidates from the ballot for whom voters have shown a clear preference, produce less experienced legislators, increase the power of unelected staffers and lobbyists, and make legislators less accountable in their last term in office.

We need not resolve this controversy to recognize that term limits, whatever their other merits, are unlikely to promote compromising mindsets conducive to governing. They are more likely to have the opposite effect. The main reason we have already noted: mutual respect necessary for compromise depends on collegial relationships that take time to cultivate. The frequent turnover caused by term limits reduces the opportunities for trust-building interactions and disrupts those that do happen to develop.

A systematic study of the Michigan legislature found that after term limits were adopted, members had fewer friendships across the aisle (though not within their own party), knew less about other members (sometimes mistaking who were chairs of certain committees), and were less civil in committee meetings (as chairs suppressed conflict instead of managing it).[26] The "shortened terms of service with a known endpoint" enabled members to "defect from compromises they [had] agreed to, to break promises, or to misrepresent...the impact of policies." Under these conditions of mutual mistrust, the few compromisers who were left—the "honest brokers" who might try "to bridge the divide between the various constituencies in the state"—could hardly be expected to succeed.[27] Even if term-limited legislators have more time for governing, the environment in which they work has less capacity for making the compromises that governing requires. We would do better to look for other ways to constrain the permanent campaign.

Rather than limiting the number of terms, increasing their length would be a more effective way to give legislators more time to govern between campaigns. Some reformers and some politicians have long favored lengthening the terms of representatives, senators, and even the president.[28] Lyndon Johnson proposed the longer terms in his State of the Union address in 1966.[29] Since then, several resolutions favoring longer terms have passed the House, though none has come close to overcoming the hurdles for passing the necessary constitutional amendment. The Constitutional Convention settled on the two-year term for House members purely as a compromise. They split the difference between Roger Sherman and Elbridge Gerry, who wanted one-year terms ("the only defense of the people against tyranny"), and James Madison, who argued for three-year terms ("necessary... for members to form any knowledge of the various interests of the States to which they do not belong").[30] Making a point that (suitably updated) resonates today, Madison objected to the shorter term because the time would be "almost consumed in preparing for and traveling to and from the seat of national business."[31] Today the problem is not travel time as such, but campaign time—which just as surely takes time away from the national business. Any reform that involves lengthening terms would need to be coupled with other measures, because the terms would still remain reasonably short (in order to hold representatives accountable) and the demands of fundraising would still remain unreasonably great (in the absence of significant campaign finance reform).

Time Is Money

By far the greatest impact of campaigning on legislators' time is fundraising. As campaigns have become more expensive, the pressure to raise money has become relentless. The money chase does not end when the election does. Almost from the first day in office, legislators begin the race for money again. Indeed, sometimes before the first day. In 2011, two would-be House members missed their swearing in because they were attending a fundraising event.[32] They later said they had taken their oath via a televised version of the ceremony—a move that did not satisfy the rules but did add to the stock of political mockery.[33] The author of an extensive review of the problem concludes: "Candidates and officeholders [have] become, in effect, full-time fundraisers... fundraising is a priority at the expense of representative democracy and the functioning of the electoral process."[34]

The time-protection argument has not figured prominently in the legal debate about campaign finance reform. The only rationale that the Supreme Court has ever accepted for regulating campaign finance is the prevention of corruption and the appearance of corruption. Democratic theorists and other reformers have put forward justifications based on the value of equality or, less commonly, on a different interpretation of the value of liberty—so far without judicial success.[35] Only recently has the time-protection rationale received serious attention and gained some judicial recognition.[36] Dissenting in a case in which the Court struck down limits in Vermont's campaign finance law, Justice Stevens wrote: "The interest in freeing candidates from the fundraising straitjacket is even more compelling... [This] has surely been confirmed by the mountains of evidence that has been accumulated in recent years concerning the time that elected officials spend raising money for future campaigns and the adverse effect of fundraising on the performance of their official duties."[37]

Proponents of the time-protection rationale point to several advantages it has over other justifications for reform (it identifies an uncontroversial objective harm, for example), but they have not emphasized its value in promoting the compromises essential to governing. To the extent that legislators are devoting time to their contributors, they have their minds on the campaign. They are locked into the uncompromising mindset.

Their most important fundraisers (those who bundle contributions) and the most influential independent groups (those that provide media support) typically expect candidates to take hardline positions and hold to them. Candidates must convince potential donors that they can be trusted to keep the faith. Not only does the time spent fundraising take time away from governing; what happens during that time reinforces attitudes that get in the way of governing. Fundraising is both an opportunity cost and also a direct cost to governing.

If these costs were more widely recognized, most politicians and most citizens would probably agree that they should be reduced if possible. But how to reduce them would remain controversial. There are abundant proposals for campaign finance reform.[38] And there are just as many obstacles to implementing them, including the Court and the Congress itself. Limits on contributions are necessary to protect the democratic process, but their effect is to force candidates to spend still more time in order to reach more donors. Limits on expenditures would better serve time-protection, but the now dominant (though misguided) interpretation of the constitutional right of free speech stands in the way.[39] With the road to limits judicially blocked, reform efforts have turned to various means of public financing.[40] The most promising are those that would encourage grassroots fundraising.[41]

Other proposed changes would apply directly to the legislature. Some reformers have called for a ban on fundraising in Congress between January and June every year, as some state legislatures do.[42] This would not raise constitutional questions. Another proposal would prohibit members from raising money outside of their districts.[43] Yet another would abolish leadership PACs, organizations set up by politicians in Congress and some state legislatures to raise money for other politicians.[44] Their purpose is hardly altruistic: the generous politicians donate because they are seeking a leadership position, a higher office, or leverage within their own party. Practices like leadership PACs extend the influence of campaigning even further, biasing the competition for leadership in the legislature, fueling partisan polarization, and multiplying the incentives to stay in the campaign mode.

For the project of protecting time for governing with a compromising mindset, we do not have to commit to any particular reform for campaign finance. What is important is to recognize that whatever reforms are proposed need to be directly targeted to the problem of the permanent campaign and its effect on compromise. Many democratic values are at risk in the current regime of campaign finance, and some reforms would be desirable quite apart from their effects on compromise. But some reforms that might help prevent corruption—for example, contribution limits without public financing—might not do much for controlling the permanent campaign. We need to recognize that a failure to deal with the problem of the permanent campaign affects the capacity not only for honest governing but for governing at all.

Primary Pressures

In addition to reducing the time politicians spend on campaigning, we might try to increase the number of politicians who are inclined to compromise to facilitate governing.[45] No one is likely to devise a test for candidates' mindsets, but our political system uses a tool— the primary—that does select for certain kinds of candidates. The type of primary affects the kind of candidate who is likely to be nominated. The more common type, the closed primary, in which only the members of a political party can vote on its nominees, favors candidates who appeal to the party's base. They are more likely to hold positions further from the center of the political spectrum and are likely to find it harder to compromise once in office.[46]

Other types of primaries give voters opportunities to influence the choice of nominees in either party. In the standard open primary, for example, a registered voter may request a ballot for any party, but then must choose among only candidates of that party. A still more open type, the blanket primary that California adopted in

1996, would permit any registered voter to vote for any nominee for any office.[47] The Supreme Court struck down California's version on the grounds that it violated the right of free association by forcing a political party to open up its candidate selection process to "persons wholly unaffiliated with the party, who may have different views from the party."[48] But the Court did not ban all open primaries. It did not rule out a nonpartisan open primary like the one used in Louisiana. In 2008, it also rejected a challenge to Washington State's novel system in which candidates themselves declare their partisan affiliation, voters may select any candidate regardless of party preference, and the two top candidates advance to the general election, regardless of their party affiliation.[49]

Although the general case for the open primary may be mixed, its contribution to a politics of compromise is clear.[50] Open primaries may not reduce the pressures of campaigning, but they encourage a different kind of campaigning and favor a different kind of candidate. They tend to produce candidates who are more centrist relative to the overall political landscape.[51] Officials elected under these systems stand closer to the median policy positions of their districts than do those elected under closed primaries. Because candidates need to "attract support from the entire electorate, not simply from members of their respective parties," they have a greater incentive to collaborate across party lines.[52] In this way, open primaries support the building of broader coalitions and reduce the factionalism that makes compromise harder.

More Participation?

Once primary time is over and politicians set out to win a general election, the pressures increase to satisfy a broader electorate. But some of the same pressure toward the partisan bases persists because the general electorate in the United States is also more tilted away from the median citizen than it needs to be. It is more difficult to register and to vote in the United States than in other Western democracies. Voter registration is not generally automatic, and Election Day is not a national holiday.[53] This electoral regime favors more activist, higher-income, and older-than-average citizens. The more difficult the simple act of voting, the more the uncompromising is favored over the compromising mindset, further decreasing the electoral incentives for politicians to compromise in office.[54] Making voting easier and declaring Election Day a holiday could ameliorate this problem.

Should we also promote political activism beyond voting? This may be a worthy aim for other democratic reasons, but by itself it is not likely to serve the cause of compromise. Political activists are not only more partisan, which is to be expected. They are also less tolerant of partisan differences and more closed-minded to compromise.[55] That is partly why some political scientists see political activism not as a remedy but as part of the problem. Institutional changes intended to give "more power to the people" have had the "perverse consequence" of transferring "influence to political activists who were not like most people...[T]heir points of view are more extreme [and] their feelings about issues are more intense."[56]

Others are prepared to take a more favorable view of activism but only if it is coupled with efforts to change the antimajoritarian structure of the American government to make it more responsive to the majority party, along the lines of British parliamentarianism. They would make a political virtue out of one-party dominance by restructuring government so that a strong partisan political movement would be capable of leading its side to a series of electoral victories so decisive that it could govern without having to compromise much.[57]

But neither partisan side of the American political spectrum, let alone the less activist and more moderate center, shows any sign of favoring the wholesale restructuring of American government that would be required. Less radical institutional changes, such as opening up the primary process or instituting citizens' assemblies, could give moderate citizens greater opportunities to participate.[58] Perhaps even moderates can be mobilized. Yet it took a late-night comedian to try. With his "Rally to Restore Sanity" Jon Stewart set out to mobilize a million moderates for a march on Washington in the fall of 2010.[59] This march was far from a political movement, and Stewart—true to his primary role as an entertainer—deliberately stopped short of calling on anyone to become more politically active.[60]

Any reform effort that seeks to promote more participation and at the same time sustain the disposition to compromise will need to look beyond political structures to social institutions such as the media and civic education.[61] We cannot count on politicians or political movements alone to make the changes surveyed here.[62] Madison presciently recognized the difficulty. We can trust the normal process of representation, he said, provided that the issue is one on which representatives share a common interest with their constituents. But we should be "jealous" of assigning representatives the final authority on those questions in which they "have a personal interest distinct from that of their constituents."[63] The qualifications clauses in Article I (referring to membership in the legislature) were his immediate concern, but he evidently intended his rule to apply to all provisions that affected both the privileges of office and the prospects for winning and retaining office. Except for proposals to lengthen terms, politicians are not inclined to favor changes to a system that has treated them well, especially changes that might put their careers at greater risk. Even politicians who would be willing to press for changes to constrain the permanent campaign cannot do the job alone. They have an increasingly difficult time gaining the support they need in a media environment that reinforces the tendency to turn governing into campaigning.

Minding the Media

No institutions beyond government and elections have contributed more to making campaigns permanent than the media. They tend to cover governing as if it were campaigning, and campaigning as if it had little to do with governing. The former tendency frustrates efforts to compromise, while the latter reinforces the resistance to compromise that hardly needs reinforcing. Sustaining both tendencies is a type of political journalism that has become dominant in recent years—so-called horse race coverage.[64] It reflects only too well the uncompromising mindset by portraying politicians as engaged in a no-holds-barred competitive struggle in which only one side can win, and neither has any reason to cooperate with the other.

In more general terms, the coverage is a form of the strategic framing of political events.[65] (The mindsets themselves, as we indicated in chapter 2, may be regarded as a form of framing.) Two leading media scholars write: "Strategic coverage of politics is endemic—whether the focus is campaigns or policy debates."[66] The magnitude and appeal of such coverage has expanded over the past half-century, as media outlets face increasingly intense competition for audience shares and advertising dollars in a world populated by many more channels of communication. Presenting politicians as engaged in winner-take-all contests may attract audiences and advertisers more easily than does describing the complex negotiations in which they engage.[67] And if the only alternative consisted of stories that demonstrate in tedious detail how compromises are hammered out among many competing policy positions and interlocking partisan perspectives, then neither audiences nor journalists would likely be willing to devote much attention to understanding the politics of compromise. But, as we point out below, there is another alternative.

First, we need to ask: If the uncompromising mindset is appropriate for campaigning, what is wrong with strategic framing in reporting on the campaigners? After all, the strategic framing in the media might simply be reflecting more or less accurately the uncompromising mindset of politicians caught up in the permanent campaign. The problem is that, as usually applied, strategic framing is too narrow. As a result, it tends to take a cynical turn that carries over to governing and hampers compromising. Journalists tend to interpret every politicians' claim to be standing on principle in narrowly strategic terms. How does the claim help the candidate's electoral chances, fundraising opportunities, or career advancement? Politicians are portrayed as using principles merely as strategies for defeating their opponents in this election, and once in office, for wooing more voters in the next.[68]

The possibility that politicians might sincerely hold principles but are willing to modify them to make the compromises necessary for governing is lost in the competitive fog that lingers from the campaign stories. Those politicians who do modify their principles once in office are promptly charged with flip-flopping, political opportunism, or just plain inconsistency. Such charges may often be valid, but the narrow strategic frame makes no allowance for when they are not. As a result, genuine efforts to compromise are painted with the same narrowly strategic brush as are manipulative efforts to continue the campaign by other means. At the same time, the talk shows feature commentators and politicians who represent extreme views or who take sharply differentiated positions. Compromisers do not make the most compelling television.

When the media assume politicians are motivated solely by a desire to win the next election and treat their policy proposals as only ploys to win votes, they cast a cynical pall over democratic politics. They make compromise and therefore governing more difficult.[69] Again, like most professionals who act for others while advancing their careers, politicians have mixed motives. They may be trying to do the best they can for a cause in which they believe while also striving to win or retain office. When motives are mixed, the media seriously distort democratic politics by framing what politicians do exclusively in terms of a competitive campaign.

Part of the treatment for this distortion would be a richer diet of reporting on the substance of policy and policymaking—the views of politicians, commentators, and experts on the costs and benefits, fairness, and other consequences of various proposals and the possible compromises. It would feature as a main course a range of answers to the key question about possible compromise: is a proposed law (or any feasible alternative) an improvement over the status quo?

We do not suggest that the media should concentrate only on the substance of policy. Such stories are often less captivating than those that recount the strategic maneuvering of politicians. Moreover, governing is itself strategic, and reporting on governing should not avoid strategic framing. But the frame need not be so narrow as to present politicians as acting only to defeat their opponents. The media could more often and more regularly adopt what we call broad strategic framing.

A broad strategic frame would lead journalists to emphasize not only how politicians are positioning themselves in the polls but also how they plan to achieve their policy goals—their policymaking strategies. This frame shifts the kinds of strategic questions the media asks: Would compromising or refusing to compromise be more likely to achieve the goals of either or both sides, and the public? What are the likely effects on relationships in the legislature and the possibility of compromises in the future? Are legislators missing opportunities for compromise or holding out for compromises that have no chance of success? Are they letting a search for common-ground agreements get in the way of making classic compromises in which everyone has to make major sacrifices? Who are their potential allies, and what are their conditions for support? These kinds of questions about governing, which are all strategically focused, can attract audiences at the same time as they inform citizens about the demands of governing in the context of a permanent campaign. Even in the campaign, such questions could remind everyone that campaigning is not an end in itself but only a prelude to governing.

How can the media be encouraged to present a more balanced picture of politics that would give the politics of governing at least equal time with the politics of campaigning? This is a formidable challenge. Journalists who may be inclined to favor this kind of reporting and commentary confront trends in a changing media environment that make their task more difficult than before.

Much of the new online media, like much of cable television news, caters to niche audiences who are less diverse in their political viewpoints than the audiences of traditional media, national newspapers, and television network news. The readership of national newspapers has declined sharply over the past two decades, and the viewership of television network news has shrunk, though less acutely; it has also aged.[70] As citizens increasingly not only live and work with like-minded people, but also read, view, tweet, and text through like-minded media, they are exposed to messages consistent with political tenacity and mistrust of partisan opponents more than to those conducive to compromise.[71]

Although television remains the place where "more people get the news" and "spend more time getting the news there than any other source," the niche sources of news on television also have multiplied.[72] These media competitors put added market pressure on television news programs to do whatever it takes to keep their audiences from migrating to other news sources. The pressures push in the direction of covering politics as a permanent campaign. The networks and talk radio that take sides are generally more profitable than those that try to present balanced coverage.

The flip side of this decline of the traditional media—the rise of new media—might seem to offer a way out because the new media increase the opportunities for exposure to diverse sources of information and commentary. Online and mobile technologies—along with the bundling of cable television packages—are making exposure to multiple news sources far easier and more common than ever before. One observable result is that "instead of replacing traditional news platforms, Americans are increasingly integrating new technologies into their news consumption habits."[73] They are also spending significantly more total time on the news and exposing themselves to more sources, which taken together provide more diversity than that of a single niche market.[74] The new online and mobile media technologies also provide means of public expression for the viewpoints of more citizens. This expansion of information and opinion sharing, debate, criticism, and mobilization provides the opportunity for broader democratic participation. All this seems positive for democracy, and in many respects it is.

However, the same expansion of segmented media carries with it a heightened challenge to citizens and journalists to learn how better to discern fact from fiction. When news sources cater to niche markets, readers and viewers find it easier to believe whatever supports their preexisting political perspectives and to disbelieve verifiable facts. This suits the uncompromising mindset perfectly. Rising to this challenge are nonprofit, nonpartisan fact-checking websites such as FactCheck.org.[75] But fact-checking services cannot make citizens want to separate political fact from fiction, or to take the time to do so.[76] This desire needs to be cultivated by the kind of cognitive and civic education that teaches not only how to tell fact from fiction but also how to engage with those with whom one disagrees.

Journalists themselves need to appreciate the mindsets that support and undermine governing, along with the importance of conveying information about the process and substance of governing. But any major changes in the way journalists cover campaigning and governing are not likely to come from more regulations or new laws restricting the media. That would not be desirable even if it were feasible. In a democracy, freedom of the press is essential for disseminating the widest range of information, analyses, and perspectives on both campaigning and governing. When the question is one of balance and emphasis in coverage, the most effective resource for reform is ultimately the professional responsibility of journalists.

Several reforms that take a constructive approach, making the most of both press freedom and journalistic responsibility, are worth considering. First of all, some of the changes proposed for improving campaign coverage could enhance governmental coverage as well.[77] For example, journalists themselves could use focus groups to gain a deeper understanding of what citizens want and need in the form of political information. They may find, as did an important study of the 1992 presidential campaign, that even if horse-race coverage attracts audiences, it is neither as "useful nor [as] interesting to the public" as other forms. In the focus groups, horse-race coverage (compared with news analysis and interviews with candidates) "provoked little discussion, did not permit individuals to bring personal experience into their conversation, and was difficult to build on as a topic for discussion and was often perceived as biased."[78] Journalists may find that there is more room than they have assumed for broader coverage, more centered on governing than campaigning styles. Journalists also could use these groups to learn how to refine their coverage of legislative politics and perhaps discover more effective ways of informing citizens about the complexities of compromises.

Another set of proposals about campaign coverage would encourage reporters to spend less time on the campaign trail and more time on other aspects of the process. This would give them a broader perspective and also allow them to develop expertise in some relevant subject, such as economics, law enforcement, or legislative politics.[79] Journalists who stay on the campaign trail would be encouraged to rotate among the candidates to temper the "jaded, know-it-all tone" and "pack journalism" that "infects too much political news."[80] Analogous changes in the way coverage of the White House and Congress is organized could help reframe the picture of governing that now is so heavily colored by the hues of campaigning.

We could also seek ways to give greater recognition to the journalists and programs that provide the kind of coverage that would promote understanding of the need for compromising in the business of governing. Such coverage does not always have to take the form of a whole program. Let us see more frequent use of a few well-chosen, incisive questions in an interview, like those that Leslie Stahl posed to John Boehner (quoted at the beginning of chapter 2). Programs such as WGBH's *Beat the Press*, which includes a segment called "Rants and Raves," could feature more raves about interviews, stories, and reporting that provide insight into the process of governing. Over the years, the Pulitzer Prizes have been awarded in some thirty categories (currently in fourteen). Why not a new category—Explanatory Reporting on Governing—that would recognize journalism that helps citizens understand better the challenges of governing, including reaching agreements and making laws in a polarized democratic polity? Few of the winners in the existing category of "explanatory reporting" wrote about government at all, and none about the role of compromise in the political process.[81]

Other proposals would reward news organizations that readers and viewers indicate they believe contribute to their political understanding. One version invites Internet users to click a box whenever they read an article that they find informative about politics.[82] The "votes" would be transmitted to a National Endowment for Journalism, which would award a grant to the organization producing the article. Another version uses "citizenship news vouchers" instead of Internet clicks.[83] Advocates of these schemes recognize the risk that the results might simply reproduce the preferences for sensationalist and simplistic stories currently expressed in many media markets, but the advocates believe that they can build enough protections to guard against abuses, and incentives to bring out the civic-minded inclinations of readers and viewers.

In any effort to right the balance between campaigning and governing in the coverage of politics, the media certainly cannot do the job alone. Their readers and viewers share the responsibility. Because "stories that 'sell' are inevitably preferred over those that may be more substantive but lacking in audience appeal," citizens can have the greatest influence on the media by paying attention to such news stories, as do the viewers of *60 Minutes*, for example.[84] With the rise of online technologies, citizens have easy access—unmediated by journalists—to the speeches and press releases of politicians, which can supplement media analyses and broaden their strategic framing.[85] By what they choose to watch and read, citizens can demonstrate that they appreciate the benefits of engagement with a variety of viewpoints and news sources. Some studies of the changing patterns of viewership suggest that more people may be responding in this way to the increase in news media and program choices.[86] But the challenge remains. For now and for the future in any endeavor to give the compromising mindset its due, the responsibility for minding the media continues to rest with everyone—journalists, politicians, and citizens.

Strengthening Civic Education

This endeavor would have a greater chance of success in the future if the schools were to give civic education a higher priority. The kind of civic education that would include an understanding of compromise and its place in democracy is not yet common.[87] Education that could further students' understanding of the role of compromise in democracy has three aims. The first is an appreciation of compromise in American political history. All history lessons become an important source of civic education when students are taught to understand and to evaluate not only the how but also the why of political compromises that shaped critically important epochs in American history. It would be important to avoid giving students a false sense that all the epic historic compromises were morally all for the better. It should be possible to help students appreciate how American democracy has been politically constructed on political compromise—while encouraging them to assess critically the particular compromises they study.

The second aim is to develop understanding of other political perspectives well enough to present competing positions in their strongest form rather than as caricatures that can be dismissed wholesale. Observing that political activists are less likely to "hear the other side" than more passive citizens, political scientist Diana Mutz points out that "there is little if any instruction given to [American] citizens in the practical skills of politics." The skills they need are not how to run campaigns but how to handle "political differences...respectfully in informal discourse" and how to be "a successful advocate of political ideas without isolating one's self from those whose ideas differ."[88]

Effective exercises in understanding other political perspectives are all the more important because American families today tend to live in ideologically homogeneous communities and send their children to schools that mirror or accentuate this homogeneity.[89] In this environment, learning to appreciate opposing positions becomes a critically important exercise in mutual respect and civic understanding more generally.[90] It does not—nor should it—guarantee willingness to compromise on any issue, but it lays an educational foundation that helps to make compromise possible whenever it is desirable, not just when the only obvious alternative is a national crisis.

The third aim is to empower students to engage in face-to-face discussions of contemporary issues in politics. This pedagogy, still somewhat controversial, has been adopted with considerable success in a number of schools.[91] An influential report sponsored by the Carnegie Foundation found that students who have "opportunities to discuss current issues in a classroom setting…tend to have greater interest in politics, improved critical thinking and communications skills, more civic knowledge, and more interest in discussing public affairs out of school."[92] Discussions are more likely to be productive if they occur in a "classroom environment that encourages analysis and critique of multiple competing viewpoints."[93]

Promoting this kind of discussion, however, is not sufficient for a robust civic education. If the teacher sees the only purpose of debating controversial issues as helping students to clarify their own values and articulate their own views more effectively, it could even be a step backward.[94] The skills cultivated by such an approach would enable students merely to become better advocates for their own preexisting positions rather than to try to be better citizens who take the perspectives of others into account, according them the consideration and respect they deserve. In a debate-oriented pedagogy, they learn how to stand tenaciously on principle but not how to accommodate others who do not share their values.

To appreciate the value of both disagreement and compromise in politics, students need to learn how to understand diverse viewpoints and also how to accommodate them in collective endeavors when necessary to improve on the status quo and make a positive difference in society. Case studies of political compromise are useful, but perhaps more effective would be exercises in which students themselves have to come to agreement on a controversial issue that collectively affects them, as legislation affects citizens. Some civic education programs choose community issues, and others select issues over which students have a real stake, such as rules governing school conduct.[95]

ഉⓈ

Campaigning is an essential part of the democratic process, but when it spills out of its natural environment and threatens the hardiness of governing, it needs to be pruned back. The mindset it breeds is hostile to governing. To control its spread, more politicians need to adopt the compromising mindset more of the time.

Politicians who combine the mindsets require both institutional and public support to succeed in democratic politics. Institutional reforms of the kind canvassed in this chapter are an important complement to recognizing the difficulty that the dominance of campaigning over governing creates for democratic compromise. Yet major institutional change in the public interest itself requires compromise, and the leaders who would bring it about will themselves have to set their minds to it. In an earlier uncompromising era, the Beatles got it just about right: "You tell me it's the institution. Well, you know. You'd better free your mind instead."

CONCLUSION

If politics is the art of the possible, compromise is the artistry of democracy. Democracy calls on politicians to resist compromise and to accept it. They may resist it more when they campaign, but they need to accept it more when they govern. Balancing these mindsets is a formidable challenge at any time, but it becomes even more so in a time of the permanent campaign. The mindset that campaigns demand—standing tenaciously on principles and mistrusting opponents—gets in the way of negotiating the deals required to pass laws in a pluralist society. It drives out the compromising mindset that governing needs—the disposition to adapt principles and respect opponents. To govern, politicians must look beyond their campaign commitments and their electoral fortunes. The compromising mindset focuses on the critical question for governing: is the proposed law better than the status quo?

In a democracy, the spirit of the laws depends on the spirit of compromise. The compromising mindset was once more prevalent than it is today. The spirit of compromise that led to the Tax Reform Act of 1986 has faded. The bipartisan group that produced that compromise consisted of strong partisans who were otherwise quite polarized in their politics. They were by no means oblivious to electoral pressures, but they were prepared to take responsibility for governing, and willing to adopt the attitudes required to fulfill it. They appreciated—and on critical occasions practiced—the public virtue of mixing the mindsets.

No doubt compromise in American democracy has been just as difficult in some periods in the past, and politics no less contentious. But whether politicians were less polarized or more cooperative in the past does not provide an answer to the question of whether we should encourage more compromise in the present. Today, as the pressures of fundraising and media attention increase, the demands of campaigning have intensified. At the same time, the need for effective government is greater and growing, as the stakes of decision making rise and the scope of law expands.

The Uses of Mindsets

The mindsets and their relation to campaigning and governing provide a perspective that highlights the imbalance that accompanies the permanent campaign. They direct our attention to arguments and attitudes that promote or impede finding a better balance. Understanding the way these mindsets work—appreciating their implicit logic, misplaced assumptions, and unintended consequences—is an essential step toward improving the capacity of a democracy to govern effectively.

Even when they have no direct causal effect on law-making, mindsets indirectly reinforce resistance to compromise or support striving for it. They provide rationalizations that either discourage politicians from facing up to the problem or encourage them to look for ways to ameliorate it. They shape how politicians justify their conduct to one another. What they say can help or hurt the prospects of compromise. Routinely questioning the motives of opponents may be psychologically satisfying, but it undermines the conditions for cultivating the mutual respect necessary for compromising in the future. More politically productive, and potentially just as satisfying, are the respectful competitive relationships that prevail when strong partisans are able to suspend their suspicion about motives and mix their mindsets to reach desirable compromises.

Political leaders and citizens alike could benefit from seeing more clearly the strengths and weaknesses of the compromising and uncompromising mindsets, and how they interact in the democratic process. The ways in which these mindsets frame disagreements are often latent and unrecognized. Bringing the latent to light enables leaders and citizens to appreciate more fully how these mindsets operate in ways conducive to campaigning or governing. As a consequence, leaders and citizens will be better equipped to recognize opportunities to craft compromises that could make better laws for everyone.

We also have identified ways that the failure to understand how mindsets work can lead to political stalemates that almost no one wants and to missed opportunities for agreements that almost everyone could accept. One way is to fail to appreciate just how vulnerable compromises are. They are easy to resist because they often reflect a mixture of conflicting principles that satisfies no one and because each side believes it could have won more if the other side had been more reasonable, or its own leaders more resolute. Furthermore, if parties to a compromise become obsessed with finding common ground or consensus solutions, they are likely to miss the chance for any compromise at all. The success of the more common, classic compromise depends on the willingness of all sides to sacrifice something to achieve a common good that improves on the status quo when common ground does not exist or cannot be found.

Another road to stalemate is especially tempting because it seems high-minded. Standing on principle is fine, sometimes admirable, but insisting that principles and their legislative implications are absolute is a prescription for deadlock. Rejecting compromise is also often a prescription for preventing progress judged by the very same principles on which the legislator claims to be standing. Letting the confusion of compromise—its inconsistent principles—block agreement often means losing the chance to enact a law that, however much of a patchwork it might be, could make everyone better off, or at least less worse off than they would have been. In contrast, the principled prudence of the compromising mindset assesses the value of a compromise compared with available alternatives. It is more likely to reveal opportunities for progress.

Failing to appreciate the role of distrust is yet another obstacle. Because in politics motives are usually suspect and bargaining leverage often uncertain, capitulating to opponents is an ever-present fear. Mutual respect is an indispensable antidote. Without it, the parties to a compromise have little reason to believe that they are getting as much as they can reasonably expect, and they cannot assure their supporters that they are not selling out. Political leaders who combine being principled partisans with cultivating close relationships with their partisan opponents bring both the intrinsic and the instrumental values of mutual respect to the table when the time for compromise is ripe. Compromises are also more broadly accepted when the parties to the process seize opportunities to demonstrate their mutual respect amid otherwise acrimonious disagreements.

Opportunities for compromise are likely to be squandered if politicians neglect the longer-term advantages of mutual respect. If they look only at the gains and losses in the particular deal in question, they will miss the broader positive consequences of compromise, which include the effect on continuing relationships with colleagues, the capacity for effective governing in the future, and the continuing vitality of the democratic process. These considerations can tip the balance toward accepting a deal that otherwise would be doubtful, as compromises by their very nature always are—simply because they entail mutual sacrifice. Paying attention to considerations such as the value of cultivating mutual respect puts the general value of compromise back into particular compromises. Politicians are more likely to give these values their due in a legislature that provides opportunities for creating and sustaining relationships that cross political divisions and continue beyond more than a few electoral cycles.

Although we have shown how the intrusion of campaigning into governing generally obstructs compromise, we have also pointed out that in special circumstances caring about campaigning can have a positive effect. The uncertainty about the electoral effects of opposition to a particular compromise—failure to avoid government default on the debt, for example—may make even legislators with otherwise uncompromising mindsets fear that they will be blamed by their constituents for blocking the particular compromise. Even when the permanent campaign dominates legislative consciousness, all is not lost for compromise. Those legislators who are finely attuned to the permanent campaign may be more likely to compromise than those who are purely ideological.

All of these and other implications of our analysis of mindsets have special relevance for legislative institutions, where relationships continue over time and agreements cover many different issues. But anyone who cares about compromise in politics more generally—or, for that matter, in any institution in which collective decisions have to be made in face of deep disagreement—needs to attend to the dynamics of compromising and uncompromising mindsets.

Doubts about Compromise

Yet some still doubt the value of promoting compromise. They raise two general objections, which point in opposing directions. One objection is that partisan gridlock is not a problem, or if it is, it is not all that serious. The other is that, although gridlock is a serious problem, compromise cannot be the remedy.

First, take those who say that we should not worry so much about the scarcity of compromise.[1] The framers of the Constitution designed the system to make change difficult, and stalemate is to be expected, even welcomed. Voters show that they do not want change to be easy because they generally choose divided government. Furthermore, many want less government and oppose new legislation, which they believe usually expands its role. Even interest groups tend to settle for keeping what they have rather than trying to get more.

Lobbyists are most successful when they are only "attempting to protect a policy that is already in place."[2]

No doubt some political changes that groups seek are not desirable, and some delay—even obstruction—is useful to force more careful and deliberative lawmaking, as the framers intended. But in our time the balance has shifted too far in favor of stasis, and at a time when the costs of delay and inaction are higher than ever. When the aggregated votes of a divided electorate create a divided government, this does not mean that the preferences of any individual voter—let alone a majority—favor political gridlock or deadlock. In fact, most American voters continue to condemn do-nothing Congresses. Even those Americans who want less government are not satisfied with the status quo. Nor could they be. It would take massive positive action to reduce the size of government, cut the deficit, and curtail government regulation.

The imperative to act and therefore to compromise is not exclusively liberal or conservative. Almost no one is satisfied with the way things are. The only reason to privilege the status quo as a general rule is the fatalistic belief that any change is bound to make things worse. In politics that is not a sustainable position. Even if the laws were to remain the same, the world would not. The effects that unchanging laws have on the world would change, probably quite radically. It did not take the debt-ceiling crisis to drive this point home to most Americans. They have been criticizing gridlock in

Congress for years. Because preserving the status quo is not a first principle, resisting compromise cannot be the first priority.

The second general objection comes from those who favor change but believe that the resistance to compromise goes deeper than mindsets or permanent campaigns. The real problem is that "we are a deeply divided nation and are likely to remain one for a long time."[3] Under these circumstances attempts to compromise are likely to result in deadlock or worse—capitulation by weaker to stronger parties. The dominance of the uncompromising mindset in Congress and the spread of campaigning into governing are on this view merely by-products of the moral disagreement that lies deep within the political culture.

This objection does not undermine the case for compromise. It is by no means obvious that the electorate rather than the political class is so deeply divided. As one commentator put it, "America is divided over the question of whether America is divided."[4] The political class may be polarized and the parties sharply differentiated, but whether or to what extent most ordinary citizens are deeply divided is a much-disputed question. Many social scientists find substantial convergence among most citizens not only on basic values but also on political issues.[5] Furthermore, even in the polarized politics and divided government of recent years, Congress has managed to pass significant legislation—much of which could be described as classic compromises.[6]

Either the divisions are not that great, or compromise is possible even in the face of such divisions.

As for the mindsets, if they were nothing more than by-products of underlying divisions, understanding how they work would still be critical to making progress under conditions of disagreement, deep or not. In earlier chapters we have pointed out the many ways in which mindsets can make a difference in effecting and in blocking compromises. The case for the compromising mindset does not depend on ending deep partisan divisions, finding common ground, or taking a side in the debate as to whether more or less political activism is, on balance, good for American democracy. To be sure, compromise would be easier if the divisions were not so deep, the common ground were more fertile, and political activists more disposed to listen to the other side. But the need for classic compromise is even greater when the polity is polarized, consensus absent, and responsible one-party government unlikely.

It is because political disagreement is fundamental and likely to persist for the foreseeable future that the need for compromise is so great. The deeper the disagreement—the larger the sacrifices required, and the stronger the mistrust generated—the greater the need for the compromising mindset. Governing may be more difficult in these circumstances, but it will become impossible if the uncompromising mindset of campaigning continues so thoroughly to dominate the political landscape.

The uncompromising mindset should not be eliminated even if it could be. Campaigning requires it. Campaigning and the uncompromising mindset are in the DNA of the democratic process. The most democratically defensible aim therefore is to find a better balance between the mindsets. That balance is currently eluding American democracy, and it is increasingly at risk in other democracies.

The Dilemma of Reform

The balance of mindsets that democracy needs would benefit from more institutional support. We have described some institutional reforms that could promote compromise in governing and help strike a better balance in the democratic process. But we also have pointed out the practical dilemma posed by institutional reform. We seem to confront a Catch-22: the institutional reforms needed to cultivate more compromising mindsets will not be adopted without the change in mindsets that is the very aim of the institutional reforms. This is because to make most institutional changes, including those needed to encourage compromise, politicians have to compromise. To enact any significant reform that would lessen the pressures of the permanent campaign, they need to exercise the compromising mindset that those pressures tend to suppress. It seems that either legislators have the mindset, in which case they do not need the reform, or they do not have it, in which case they will not be able to enact the reform. To the extent that the uncompromising mindset dominates in the permanent campaign, the reforms needed to achieve a better balance between mindsets cannot be enacted.

The situation is not so hopeless as this statement of the dilemma might suggest. Reform often can get started if only some politicians adopt the compromising mindset. As we have seen, even in the era of the permanent campaign some politicians manage to mix the mindsets, including some of the strongest partisans. While most of the time they act as strong, principled partisans, they also are willing to compromise when necessary to improve on the status quo and when they can find partners among their partisan opponents. To the extent that these politicians can lead a bipartisan group to enact some procedural reforms that would be conducive to the compromising mindset, they can increase institutional incentives for other politicians to mix—and to this extent, better balance—the competing mindsets.

Compromising on institutional procedures is not the same as compromising on legislation, but it is no less challenging. Both kinds of compromises are easier when partisan opponents are uncertain who is more likely to win more or sacrifice less. Both kinds are harder to the extent that they threaten the electoral prospects of legislative members. It is easy to get bipartisan agreement on campaign finance reform when the effect is to preserve the current system against challengers. There is no need for compromise at all. But for most institutional reforms, including those that would facilitate compromise, the need for compromise is just as great as for most policy changes.

That compromise is necessary for reforms to encourage compromise is another reason we have emphasized the importance of understanding the mindsets. Reform is more likely to advance with a better appreciation of the dynamics of the dispositional and cognitive obstacles to compromise. It would help if both politicians and citizens better understood how an uncompromising mindset obscures the value of compromise, how a compromising mindset reveals opportunities for it, and how mixing the mindsets provides a clearer choice between alternatives that might otherwise be prematurely dismissed. It would also help if politicians developed a stronger appreciation of the political power of cultivating trusting relationships with opponents that can redound to both their partisan and the public good. Understanding how uncompromising dispositions obscure politically promising possibilities would better enable politicians to make the changes that could encourage compromise when democracy requires it.

The Support of Citizens

Even politicians who are willing to compromise to advance worthy causes will not be elected or reelected if citizens do not understand and appreciate the value of compromise and the obstacles to achieving it. Reaching out in multiple ways to citizens is a priority, because politicians cannot do the job alone. It would be futile for citizens to do nothing but say: "Politician, heal thyself." Citizens need to support politicians when they attempt to make necessary compromises and to rebuke them when they do not. They need to set their minds to voting the uncompromising out of office and to not voting in another equally uncompromising set.

We reject conceptions of democracy that either would rely on elites acting alone to balance their mindsets or would give up on compromise altogether on the slim chance that one party could gain such supermajority power that there would be no need for bipartisan compromise. Even then, there would be plenty of work for the compromising mindset within the party itself.

Politicians must be given the opportunity to govern without having to look over their shoulder every moment to check the polls and plan the next campaign. But they cannot govern responsibly without the criticism and support of citizens who appreciate what responsible governing is. Citizens should engage in political backseat driving. Their mindsets are at least as important as those of political leaders. If citizens do not appreciate the need for compromise in governing, it is even less likely that politicians will.

Governing calls on leaders to mix mindsets—to establish a balance between mistrusting and respecting opponents, and between tenaciously standing on principles and adapting them to improve on the status quo. Establishing this balance is as essential to democracy as it is difficult. Leaders who compete when appropriate and cooperate when necessary can succeed in governing. But they can succeed only if they have the support of citizens who themselves appreciate the role that the mindsets of compromise play in democracy.

Notes

Introduction

1. Hugh Heclo, "Campaigning and Governing: A Conspectus," in *The Permanent Campaign and Its Future*, ed. Norman Ornstein and Thomas Mann (Washington, DC: American Enterprise Institute, 2000), 37. The term "permanent campaign" was given currency by the journalist Sidney Blumenthal in his book on the Reagan presidency, *The Permanent Campaign* (New York: Simon and Schuster, 1982). The phenomenon, though not always described with the same terms or in the same way, has been prominent in the work of several political scientists, including David Mayhew, *Congress: The Electoral Connection* (New Haven, CT: Yale University Press, 1974); Samuel Kernell, *Going Public: New Strategies of Presidential Leadership* (Washington, DC: Congressional Quarterly, 1993); Anthony King, *Running Scared: Why America's Politicians Campaign Too Much and Govern Too Little* (New York: Routledge, 1997); and Charles O. Jones, *Passages to the Presidency: From Campaigning to Governing* (Washington, DC: Brookings Institution Press, 1998). A valuable collection of essays on the significance of the permanent campaign and the possibilities for limiting it in contemporary American politics is Ornstein and Mann, *The Permanent Campaign*.

2. See the essays in Ornstein and Mann, *The Permanent Campaign*.

3. It is sometimes suggested that whether the "campaign style of governing" is a "positive development for democracy" turns on whether one adopts a trustee or delegate theory of representation. "The trustee preserves the distinction between campaigning and governing; delegates are ... seeking throughout their service to mirror the interests and concerns of their constituents" (Jones, *Passages to the Presidency*, 196–97). But on any democratic trustee theory, leaders must take into account the effect of their decisions on the

next election, and on any defensible delegate theory, leaders must have sufficient time to try to carry out the policies favored by their constituents before being held accountable.

4. A summary prepared by the staff of the Joint Committee on Taxation (July 14, 1986) is available at http://www.archive.org/details/summaryofhr3838t1486unit.

5. We follow the now-standard practice of using the shortened title, the Affordable Care Act. The health-care reform legislation actually consists of two separate acts: the Patient Protection and Affordable Care Act, the Senate version passed by the House and signed into law on March 23, 2010, and the Health Care and Education Reconciliation Act, intended to meet objections of House members and signed into law on March 30. The latter consists entirely of revisions and is unintelligible on its own. A document that consolidates the two was prepared by the House Office of Legislative Counsel and contains the full text of the reform, though the document itself does not have the status of law. It is available at http://www.ncsl.org/documents/health/ppaca-consolidated.pdf.

6. Our account relies on Jeffrey Birnbaum and Alan Murray, *Showdown at Gucci Gulch* (New York: Vintage Books, 1988); Randall Strahan, "Members' Goals and Coalition-Building Strategies in the US House: The Case of Tax Reform," *Journal of Politics* 51, no. 2 (1989): 373–84; Timothy J. Conlan, Margaret T. Wrightson, and David R. Beam, *Taxing Choices: The Politics of Tax Reform* (Washington, DC: Congressional Quarterly Press, 1989); and John F. Witte, "The Tax Reform Act of 1986: A New Era in Tax Politics?," *American Politics Research* 19, no. 4 (1991): 438–57.

7. "Speech Given July 19: Mondale Accepts Presidential Nomination," *Congressional Quarterly Weekly* (July 21, 1984), 1792–94.

8. Witte, "Tax Reform Act of 1986," 440.

9. Our account draws on Staff of the *Washington Post*, *Landmark: The Inside Story of America's New Health-Care Law and What It Means for Us All* (New York: PublicAffairs Books, 2010); Jonathan Alter, *The Promise: President Obama, Year One* (New York: Simon and Schuster, 2010), 244–66, 395–421; and Jacob S. Hacker, "The Road to Somewhere: Why Health Reform Happened, or Why Political Scientists Who Write about Public Policy Shouldn't Assume They Know How to Shape It," *Perspectives on Politics* 8, no. 4 (2010): 861–76.

10. Staff of the *Washington Post*, *Landmark*, chap. 1.

11. Our approach treats compromise both as process and outcome. For an analysis that brings out this dual nature of compromise

and its foundation in mutual respect, see Arthur Kuflik, "Morality and Compromise," in *NOMOS XXI: Compromise in Ethics, Law and Politics*, ed. J. Roland Pennock and John W. Chapman (New York: New York University Press, 1979), 38–65. For the difference between compromising and the related concept of settling, see Robert Goodin, *On Settling* (Princeton, NJ: Princeton University Press, 2012).

12. Trimmers may not deserve the negative reputation they have long endured. See Cass Sunstein, "Trimming," *Harvard Law Review* 122, no. 4 (2009): 1049–94.

13. Henry Richardson proposes a similar distinction but develops it as a contrast between means and ends. He distinguishes "bare compromise," which involves a "willingness to accept a less satisfactory means to the ends one started with," and "deep compromise," which requires a "reconsideration of what is worth seeking for its own sake…a change in one's ends" (*Democratic Autonomy: Public Reasoning about the Ends of Policy* [Oxford: Oxford University Press, 2002], 144–61; quote on 146–47). He devotes more attention to deep compromise, which (we agree) is a worthy democratic ideal, and the pursuit of which can support mutual respect. But the "willingness" of bare compromise also supports mutual respect, is more common, and no less important.

14. Matt Viser, "Romney Calls for Common Ground," *Boston Globe*, August 16, 2011.

15. Alan Simpson and Erskine Bowles, "Our Advice to the Debt Supercommittee: Go Big, Be Bold, Be Smart," *Washington Post*, September 30, 2011. Cf. David Brooks, "Bigger Is Easier," *New York Times*, December 16, 2010: It may be "easier to push through big change by marrying the left and the right than by relying upon an unfortunately weak vital center."

16. Peter J. Carnevale, "Creativity in the Outcomes of Conflict," in *Handbook of Conflict Resolution*, ed. Morton Deutsch and Peter T. Coleman, 2nd ed. (San Francisco: Jossey-Bass, 2006), 414–35; Roger Fisher and William L. Ury, *Getting to YES: Negotiating Agreement Without Giving In* (Boston: Houghton Mifflin, 1981); James K. Sebenius, "Negotiation Analysis: A Characterization and Review," *Management Science* 38, no. 1 (1992): 18–38; and Richard Walton and Robert McKersie, *A Behavioral Theory of Labor Negotiations* (Ithaca, NY: ILR Press, 1965).

17. Mary Parker Follett, "Constructive Conflict," in *Dynamic Administration: The Collected Papers of Mary Parker Follett*, ed. E. M. Fox and L. Urwick (London: Pitman, 1973), 1–20.

18. Gerald B. Wetlaufer, "The Limits of Integrative Bargaining," in *What's Fair? Ethics for Negotiators*, ed. Carrie Menkel-Meadow and Michael Wheeler (San Francisco: Jossey-Bass, 2004), 30–56.

19. Alter, *The Promise*, 249.

20. Compare Alan I. Abramowitz, *The Disappearing Center: Engaged Citizens, Polarization, and American Democracy* (New Haven, CT: Yale University Press, 2010); Morris P. Fiorina and Samuel J. Abrams, "Political Polarization in the American Public," *Annual Review of Political Science* 11 (2008): 563–88; and Morris P. Fiorina, with Samuel J. Abrams and Jeremy C. Pope, *Culture War? The Myth of a Polarized America*, 3rd ed. (New York: Longman, 2010). Also see Nolan McCarty, Keith Poole, and Howard Rosenthal, *Polarized America: The Dance of Ideology and Unequal Riches* (Cambridge, MA: MIT Press, 2008); and Ronald Brownstein, *The Second Civil War: How Extreme Partisanship Has Paralyzed Washington and Polarized America* (New York: Penguin Press, 2007).

21. Abramowitz, *The Disappearing Center*, 170. On the relationship between segregated living patterns and polarization, see Bill Bishop, *The Big Sort: Why the Clustering of Like-Minded America Is Tearing Us Apart* (Boston: Houghton Mifflin, 2008).

22. Abramowitz, *The Disappearing Center*, 170.

23. Kuflik, "Morality and Compromise," 38–65; and J. Patrick Dobel, *Compromise and Political Action* (Savage, MD: Rowman and Littlefield, 1990), 79–99.

24. Joseph H. Carens, "Compromise in Politics," in *NOMOS XXI: Compromise in Ethics, Law and Politics*, ed. J. Roland Pennock and John W. Chapman (New York: New York University Press, 1979), 123–41; quote on 139.

CHAPTER 1: VALUING COMPROMISE

1. Pew Research Center, "Broad Support for Political Compromise in Washington: But Many Are Hesitant to Yield on Contentious Issues" (Washington, DC: Pew Research Center, January 22, 2007), 11–13.

2. Ibid., 12.

3. In a 2011 survey, "54% say they like elected officials who stick to their positions, while 40% prefer elected officials who make compromises with people they disagree with." Among Tea Party supporters, 69 percent preferred elected officials who stick to their positions. Pew Research Center, "Few Are Angry at Government, but

Discontent Remains High" (Washington, DC: Pew Research Center, March 3, 2011), 1.

4. In surveys starting in 2010, long-standing support among Republicans and Democrats for the general idea of compromise began to erode as acrimonious fights over particular issues, such as health care, taxation, and government spending became generalized into a grand battle about the role of government. The midterm electoral campaigns of 2010 seem to have been the turning point, when 49 percent said they most admire political leaders who stick to their positions without compromising, while 42 percent said that they most admire political leaders who make compromises with people they disagree with. Pew Research Center, "Little Compromise on Compromising" (Washington, DC: Pew Research Center, September 20, 2010). Also see Pew Research Center, "Few Are Angry at Government, but Discontent Remains High."

5. Pew Research Center, "Broad Support for Political Compromise in Washington," 14.

6. A Gallup poll in 2011 asked Americans whether they would like the members who represented their views on the bipartisan "supercommittee" charged with coming up with a plan to reduce the federal deficit to either "hold out for the plan you agree with even if it prevents the committee from reaching an agreement," or "agree to [a] compromise plan, even if it is a plan you disagree with." Six out of ten Americans—including a majority of Republicans, independents, and Democrats—favored compromise on a plan, even if they expected to disagree with it. The distribution was 55 percent of Republicans, 57 percent of independents, and 67 percent of Democrats. Frank Newport, "Americans Want New Debt Supercommittee to Compromise: Only Tea Party Supporters Take Hard-Line Stance," Gallup Poll report, August 10, 2011, http://www.gallup.com/poll/148919/americans-new-debt-supercommittee-compromise.aspx.

7. Among major self-identified partisan groups, supporters of the Tea Party are the most opposed to compromise, but even they are not steadfast in their opposition to it. By mid-July 2011, three months after a large majority of Tea Party supporters said they opposed budget compromise, a similarly large majority (almost two-thirds) said they thought Republicans in Congress should compromise in order to come to an agreement with Democrats to raise the debt ceiling. When presented with the choice of whether an agreement should include only spending cuts, tax increases, or a combination of both, a majority of Tea Party supporters said that it should include a

combination of spending cuts and tax increases. Results are from a July 2011 nationwide CBS News poll reported by Kate Zernike, "That Monolithic Tea Party Just Wasn't There," *New York Times*, August 2, 2011.

8. Here is a sample of criticisms from a range of political perspectives: Maya MacGuineas of the Committee for a Responsible Federal Budget, criticizing the deal for not cutting the nation's debt enough and slowing its growth (http://www.nytimes.com/2011/08/03/us/politics/03spend.html?_r=2&h); Ruy Teixeira of the Center for American Progress: "The debt ceiling deal has been struck and the score looks to be in the neighborhood of Republicans: a zillion, Democrats: zero" (http://www.tnr.com/article/politics/93041/obama-independent-voters); and Fareed Zakaria: "[W]hat the deal does is kick tough choices down the road..." (http://www.fareedzakaria.com/home/Articles/Entries/2011/8/4_The_Debt_Deals_Failure.html).

9. Thomas Vernor Smith, "Compromise: Its Context and Limits," *Ethics* 53, no. 1 (1942): 1–13; quote on 2.

10. Ibid., 13. Smith evidently intended this proposal as a sardonic criticism of overly conscientious citizens who do not recognize the need for compromise. But, as we show, a different kind of division of labor—between the roles for the compromising and uncompromising mindsets—is a desirable feature of the democratic process. An early version of this argument can be detected in a somewhat cryptic form in *On Compromise* by the nineteenth-century theorist and statesman John Morley (London: MacMillan, 1908). See especially his discussion of the "three independent provinces of compromise," 94–95.

11. Edmund Burke, "On Conciliation with the Colonies," in *Speeches and Letters on American Affairs* (London: Dent, 1908), 130–31.

12. Edmund Burke, "Speech to the Electors of Bristol," November 3, 1774, in *The Founders' Constitution*, ed. Philip B. Kurland and Ralph Lerner (Chicago: University of Chicago Press, 1987), 1:391–92.

13. Dennis F. Thompson, "Mill in Parliament: When Should a Philosopher Compromise?," in *J. S. Mill's Political Thought*, ed. Nadia Urbinati and Alex Zakaras (Cambridge: Cambridge University Press, 2007), 166–99.

14. Pew Research Center, "Broad Support for Political Compromise in Washington," 15.

15. E.g., Paul Ricœur, "Pour une éthique du compromis," *Alternatives Non Violentes* 80 (1991): 2–7, esp. 3.

16. This defense of compromise could be regarded as "pragmatic" in the broad sense stipulated by Simon Căbulea May, who argues that "moral compromise in political life is only ever warranted for pragmatic reasons." But he also argues that those pragmatic reasons must be morally constrained in various ways ("Principled Compromise and the Abortion Controversy," *Philosophy & Public Affairs* 33, no. 4 [2005]: 317, 322–23). In our view, mutual respect in a democracy provides some of those moral constraints, but it does not provide a sufficient reason to compromise, nor does it give compromise an independent intrinsic value. The general value of compromise, as we defend it here, does not alone determine whether the content of any particular compromise is acceptable.

17. David Brady and Morris Fiorina, "Congress in the Era of the Permanent Campaign," in *The Permanent Campaign and Its Future*, ed. Norman Ornstein and Thomas Mann (Washington, DC: American Enterprise Institute, 2000), 154–55.

18. James Madison, Federalist No. 10, in *The Federalist*, ed. Jacob E. Cooke (Middletown, CT: Wesleyan University Press, 1961), 59.

19. Mutual respect and reciprocity play a prominent role in theories of deliberative democracy: see Amy Gutmann and Dennis Thompson, *Why Deliberative Democracy?* (Princeton, NJ: Princeton University Press, 2004), 95–124, 151–56; and Gutmann and Thompson, *Democracy and Disagreement* (Cambridge, MA: Harvard University Press, 1996), 52–55, 79–91. But many other theorists also emphasize the importance of a principle of reciprocity (and by implication the value of mutual respect), including Corey Brettschneider, *Democratic Rights: The Substance of Self-Government* (Princeton, NJ: Princeton University Press, 2010), 34–37; Ronald Dworkin, *Is Democracy Possible Here?* (Princeton, NJ: Princeton University Press, 2008), 5, 64, 112, 132–33; Carol C. Gould, *Rethinking Democracy: Freedom and Social Cooperation in Politics, Economy, and Society* (Cambridge: Cambridge University Press, 1988), 31–90; John Rawls, *A Theory of Justice* (Cambridge, MA: Harvard University Press, 1999), 29–30, 155–56, 437–49; and Rawls, *Political Liberalism* (New York: Columbia University Press, 1996), 16–22, 49–54.

20. George Santayana, *Soliloquies in England and Later Soliloquies* (New York: Charles Scribner's Sons, 1923), 83 (emphasis added). He goes on to say: "[T]o the inner man, to the profound Psyche within us, whose life is warm, nebulous and plastic, compromise seems the path of profit and justice." The comment occurs in an essay urging a more ecumenical attitude toward religion in England.

21. As Frances Kamm explains, a compromise "connotes some bottom line that does not represent the complex truth, but gives weight to conflicting factors despite the fact that doing so does not lead to the truth." It should be distinguished from both a "construction of corrected principles which gives proper weight to different morally relevant factors" and from "the dominance of one value with a negative residue" ("The Philosopher as Insider and Outsider," *Journal of Medicine & Philosophy* 15, no. 4 [1990]: 347–74; quote on 363). Also see, on the "paradox of compromise," David Luban, "Bargaining and Compromise: Recent Work on Negotiation and Informal Justice," *Philosophy & Public Affairs* 14, no. 4 (1985): 414–16.

22. David M. Herszenhorn, "Bush Signs Sweeping Housing Bill," *New York Times*, July 30, 2008.

23. Jennifer Steinhauer, "Farm Subsidies Become Target amid Spending Cuts," *New York Times*, May 6, 2011.

24. John Rawls, *Justice as Fairness* (Cambridge, MA: Harvard University Press, 2003), 32–38.

25. U.S. House of Representatives, Committee on Ways and Means, *Summary of Welfare Reforms Made by Public Law 104-193: The Personal Responsibility and Work Opportunity Reconciliation Act and Associated Legislation*, 104th Cong., 2nd sess., November 6, 1996 (Washington, DC: Government Printing Office, 1996).

26. Its success was undoubtedly aided by other legislative changes, such as a significant increase in the minimum wage, expansion of the Earned Income Tax Credit, and a decrease in the unemployment rate as the economy boomed in the last half of the 1990s. As Rebecca Blank writes, "In many ways, the late 1990s were the best time imaginable to enact and implement work-oriented welfare reform" ("Evaluating Welfare Reform in the United States," *Journal of Economic Literature* 40, no. 4 [December 2002]: 1105–66.) Also see Jeffrey A. Frankel and Peter R. Orszag, eds., *American Economic Policy in the 1990s* (Cambridge, MA: MIT Press, 2002).

27. Robert Kuttner, "Comment: Why Liberals Need Radicals," *American Prospect*, May 22, 2000, 4. Also see Ta-Nehisi Coates, "Obama and His Discontents," *New York Times*, July 28, 2011: "Obama would do well to understand that while democracy depends on intelligent compromise, it also depends on the ill-tempered gripers and groaners out in the street."

28. See, for example, Charles Tilly and Sidney Tarrow, *Contentious Politics* (Boulder, CO: Paradigm Publishers, 2006). The classic theoretical statement of the value of contention is John Stuart Mill's *On Liberty* (John Stuart Mill, *Collected Works: XVIII. Essays*

on *Politics and Society*, volume 18, ed. J. M. Robson [London: Routledge and Kegan Paul, 1977]). Some recent democratic theorists have presented a more radical appreciation of contentious politics or, in their terms, of the need "to come to terms with 'the political' in its antagonistic dimension" (Chantal Mouffe, *The Democratic Paradox* [London: Verso, 2009], 129).

29. Kate Zernike, *Boiling Mad: Inside Tea Party America* (New York: Times Books, 2010); Jill Lepore, *The Whites of Their Eyes: The Tea Party's Revolution and the Battle over American History* (Princeton, NJ: Princeton University Press, 2010); and Theda Skocpol and Vanessa Williamson, *The Tea Party and the Remaking of Republican Conservatism* (New York: Oxford University Press, 2012).

30. Poll Watch Daily, "Many Democratic Liberals Want Obama to Challenge GOP More," April 19, 2011, http://www.pollwatchdaily .com/tag/john-boehner/. Also see Pew Research Center, "Little Compromise on Compromising."

31. Senator Rand Paul (R-KY), "The Budget," *Congressional Record* 157, issue 55 (April 14, 2011), S2481–82.

32. Vanessa Williamson, Theda Skocpol, and John Coggin, "The Tea Party and the Remaking of Republican Conservatism," *Perspectives on Politics* 9, no. 1 (2011): 25–43; quote on 36.

33. Ibid., 36–37. For an early account of how reforms in the nominating processes in the 1960s gave rise to amateur party activists who were more uncompromisingly ideological (then on the left, and only later on the right) and less oriented toward governing than toward criticizing government, see James Q. Wilson, *The Amateur Democrat: Club Politics in Three Cities* (Chicago: University of Chicago Press, 1966).

34. Zernike, "That Monolithic Tea Party Just Wasn't There."

35. Ibid.

36. Carl Hulse, "After Health Vote, Threats on Democrats," *New York Times*, March 24, 2010.

37. Dennis F. Thompson, "Representing Future Generations: Political Presentism and Democratic Trusteeship," *Critical Review of International Social and Political Philosophy* 13, no. 1 (March 2010): 17–37.

38. John Gray, "Communists and Nazis: Just as Evil?," *New York Review of Books*, April 8, 2010, 1–9.

39. David M. Herszenhorn, "No Thanks, Ben Nelson Says," *New York Times*, January 16, 2010.

40. Jeffrey Birnbaum and Alan Murray, *Showdown at Gucci Gulch* (New York: Vintage Books, 1988), 258–59.

41. Ibid., 259, 271.

42. Senator Bob Casey, "New Health Reform Pro-Life Law," *Scranton Times-Tribune*, April 4, 2010, http://thetimes-tribune.com/opinion/editorials-columns/guest-columnists/new-health-reform-pro-life-law-1.715275#axzz1LDwmRR31.

43. Jay Newton-Small, "Can a Pro-Life Dem Bridge the Health-Care Divide?," *Time*, November 24, 2009, http://www.time.com/time/politics/article/0,8599,1942614,00.html.

44. We draw on the account in Jack Rakove, *Original Meaning: Politics and Ideas in the Making of the Constitution* (New York: Random House, 1996), 57–93.

45. Ibid., 93.

46. Ibid.

47. Ibid.

48. The counterfactual questions are all from Rakove, ibid.

49. Ibid.

50. For the most influential formulation of the problem, see Michael Walzer, "Political Action: The Problem of Dirty Hands," *Philosophy & Public Affairs* 2 (Winter 1973): 160–80.

51. As Chiara Lepora argues, "Compromising may be a good choice, all things considered, even taking into account all the additional pro tanto wrongs for which you become responsible in the course of compromising...But the pro tanto wrongs are only counterbalanced, not cancelled. They remain on the scale, as a justified source of moral discomfort" (*Journal of Philosophy*, 20, no. 1 [2011]: 1–22; quote on 22). However, we do not follow Lepora's view that intrapersonal compromise ("adjudicating among our own conflicting values") is a necessary condition of interpersonal compromises. Adjudicating among your own values typically involves a conflict between values you affirm, whereas compromising with an opponent involves a conflict between values you affirm and values you would reject if you could.

52. William E. Nelson, "Reason and Compromise in the Establishment of the Federal Constitution, 1787–1801," *William and Mary Quarterly*, 3rd ser., 44, no. 3 (1987): 458–84.

53. Quoted by Nelson, ibid., 463.

54. James Madison, *Notes of Debates in the Federal Convention of 1787*, 2nd ed., entry for May 29 (Athens: Ohio University Press, 1985), 28.

55. Nelson, "Reason and Compromise in the Establishment of the Federal Constitution," 465.

56. Michael Allen Gillespie, "Massachusetts: Creating Consensus," in *Ratifying the Constitution*, ed. Michael Allen Gillespie and Michael Lienesch (Lawrence: University Press of Kansas, 1989), 138–69; Cecil L. Eubanks, "New York: Federalism and the Political Economy," in idem, 300–341; and Rakove, *Original Meaning*, 121, 126–27.

57. H. L. Mencken, "Mr. Mencken Sounds Off," *Life Magazine*, August 5, 1946, 4.

58. Ronald Reagan, *An American Life* (New York: Simon and Schuster, 1999), 171.

CHAPTER 2: RESISTING COMPROMISE

1. CBS, *60 Minutes*, "Meet the Next House Speaker, Rep. John Boehner," December 12, 2010, http://www.cbsnews.com/stories/2010/12/09/60minutes/main7134156_page3.shtml?tag=cont entMain;contentBody.

2. We concentrate on these characteristics because of their close connection to the political process. They are not, of course, the only attitudes that obstruct compromise. The literature on negotiation is replete with examples of approaches that discourage agreement, as well as techniques to mitigate them. For a sample of "cognitive errors that people make in negotiations," including framing effects, see Simone Moran and Ilana Ritov, "Valence Framings in Negotiations," in *Perspectives on Framing*, ed. Gideon Keren (New York: Psychology Press, 2010), 239–54.

3. Gerd Bohner and Nina Dickel, "Attitudes and Attitude Change," *Annual Review of Psychology* 62 (2011): 391–417; quote on 394.

4. Dennis Chong and James N. Druckman, "Framing Theory," *Annual Review of Political Science* 10 (2007): 103–26; James N. Druckman, "What's It All About? Framing in Political Science," in *Perspectives on Framing*, 279–301; and Brian F. Schaffner and Patrick J. Sellers, eds., *Winning with Words: The Origins and Impact of Political Framing* (New York: Routledge, 2010). Also see Porismita Borah, "Conceptual Issues in Framing Theory: A Systematic Examination of a Decade's Literature," *Journal of Communication* 61, no. 2 (2011): 246–63. Although most of this work in political science stands closer to psychology than to other social sciences, the seminal work in this century is by an anthropologist and a sociologist.

See Gregory Bateson, *Steps to an Ecology of Mind* (1955; repr., Chicago: University of Chicago Press, 2000), 187–89; and Irving Goffman, *Frame Analysis* (New York: Harper and Row, 1974).

5. Chong and Druckman, "Framing Theory," 105–6.

6. Chong and Druckman maintain that priming—"changes in the standards that people use to make political evaluations"—is sufficiently similar to framing that "the two terms can be used interchangeably" (ibid., 115).

7. Druckman, "What's It All About?," 287.

8. Dennis Chong and James N. Druckman, "A Theory of Framing and Opinion Formation in Competitive Elite Environments," *Journal of Communication* 57 (2007): 99–118.

9. Unfortunately, the research is not much help with the obvious question: "Why are some frames perceived as strong and others as weak? Even the large persuasion literature offers scant insight" (Druckman, "What's It All About?," 294).

10. James N. Druckman and Kjersten R. Nelson, "Framing and Deliberation: How Citizens' Conversations Limit Elite Influence," *American Journal of Political Science* 47, no. 4 (2003): 729–45.

11. In the literature on framing, equivalency or valence effects are distinguished from issue or emphasis effects (Chong and Druckman, "Framing Theory," 114). The former are logically equivalent or materially identical descriptions (for example, 90 percent employment/10 percent unemployment) that produce different responses. These are better known thanks to the work of Daniel Kahneman and Amos Tversky (e.g., "Choices, Values, and Frames," *American Psychologist* 39, no. 4 [1984]: 341–50). The latter effects (issues or emphasis) refer to qualitatively different yet potentially relevant considerations (e.g., free speech v. public safety), which also may produce different responses depending on the frame. They are the more common type in public opinion research and are more closely related to the concept of mindset as we use it. But see Shanto Iyengar, "Framing Research: The Next Steps," in *Winning with Words*, 185–91.

12. Representative Tom DeLay (R-TX), "Resignation as Member of Committee on Appropriations," *Congressional Record* 152, issue 72 (June 8, 2006), H3548–50. DeLay acknowledged that "politics demands compromise, and,... even the most partisan among us have to understand that," but he emphasized that "we must never forget that compromise and bipartisanship are means, not ends, and are properly employed only in the service of higher principles."

13. Edmund Burke, "Speech to the Electors of Bristol," November 3, 1774, in *The Founders' Constitution*, ed. Philip B. Kurland and Ralph Lerner (Chicago: University of Chicago Press, 1987), 1:391–92.

14. Ibid.

15. Burke, "On Conciliation with the Colonies," in *Speeches and Letters on American Affairs* (London: Dent, 1908), 130–31.

16. Robert Paul Wolff, "Beyond Tolerance," in *A Critique of Pure Tolerance*, by Robert Paul Wolff, Barrington Moore Jr., and Herbert Marcuse (Boston: Beacon Press, 1965), 21.

17. "Focus on interests, not positions" is perhaps the most common formulation, but "positions" is ambiguous in the literature, sometimes meaning commitments and values, sometimes simply a concrete proposal. See Chris Provis, "Interests vs. Positions: A Critique of the Distinction," *Negotiation Journal* 12, no. 4 (1996): 305–23.

18. For a discussion that presents a distinction between compromises of principles and interests (concluding that some of the former are acceptable), see Theodore M. Benditt, "Compromising Interests and Principles," in *NOMOS XXI: Compromise in Ethics, Law and Politics*, ed. J. Roland Pennock and John W. Chapman (New York: New York University Press, 1979), 26–37.

19. Michael Ignatieff, "Getting Iraq Wrong," *New York Times Magazine*, August 5, 2007, 26. But he adds: "Knowing the difference between a good and a bad compromise is more important in politics than holding onto pure principle at any price. A good compromise restores the peace and enables both parties to go about their business with some element of their vital interest satisfied."

20. See Martin Benjamin, *Splitting the Difference: Compromise and Integrity in Ethics and Politics* (Lawrence: University Press of Kansas, 1990). Setting aside the title of the book, we regard Benjamin's criteria for an "integrity-preserving compromise" as consistent with the concept of the compromising mindset. They include the parties' commitment to mutual tolerance and reasonable uncertainty of the disputed positions, owing to the moral complexity of the issue (32–45).

21. Avishai Margalit, *On Compromise and Rotten Compromises* (Princeton, NJ: Princeton University Press, 2009), 39.

22. Ibid., 2.

23. Margalit's criteria for "sanguine compromises" (for example, "recognizing the point of view of the other") may be intended to

provide a way of distinguishing better and worse "decent compromises" (ibid., 41–54). But the criteria refer to the process more than to the content of the compromise, and in any case they are not unconditional, as his cruelty and humiliation standard is.

24. As the emphasis in the research on negotiation has shifted in recent years toward more descriptive approaches, the studies have shown that outcomes cannot usually be predicted by formal criteria such as Pareto-optimality and that they are determined by a much wider range of variables than had been earlier assumed. See Leigh Thompson, Jiunwen Wang, and Brian C. Gunia, "Negotiation," *Annual Review of Psychology* 61 (2010): 491–515.

25. Ronald Dworkin, *Law's Empire* (Cambridge, MA: Harvard University Press, 1986), 176.

26. Ibid., 179.

27. Ibid., 178.

28. For a nuanced criticism of "internal" compromises, see Samantha Besson, *The Morality of Conflict: Reasonable Disagreement and the Law* (Oxford: Oxford University Press; Portland, OR: Hart Publishing, 2005), 257–84.

29. Dworkin, *Law's Empire*, 436n.8.

30. Ibid., 178, 184–86, 436n.9.

31. Ibid., 183–84 (emphasis added).

32. See Jane Mansbridge et al., "The Place of Self-Interest and the Role of Power in Deliberative Democracy," *Journal of Political Philosophy* 18, no. 1 (2010): 64–100. Cf. Jürgen Habermas: "... compromises make up the bulk of political processes" ("Three Normative Models of Democracy," *Constellations* 1, no. 1 [December 1994]: 1–10; quote on 5).

33. Amy Gutmann and Dennis Thompson, *Why Deliberative Democracy?* (Princeton, NJ: Princeton University Press, 2004), 6–7, 57–59, 110–19.

34. For a distinction between cynicism and skepticism, along with evidence showing that media coverage of politics reinforces cynicism about electoral politics, see Joseph N. Cappella and Kathleen Hall Jamieson, *Spiral of Cynicism: The Press and the Public Good* (New York: Oxford University Press, 1997), 25–26 and passim.

35. Jacob S. Hacker, "The Road to Somewhere," *Perspectives on Politics* 8, no. 4 (2010): 861–76; quote on 871 (emphasis added).

36. Katharine Q. Seelye, "Questioning Motives," *New York Times*, August 18, 2009. (Seelye calls the ads "misleading.")

37. John Boehner, "Taxpayer-Funded Abortion Is Not Health-Care Reform," *National Review Online*, July 23, 2009, http://www

.nationalreview.com/critical-condition/48614/taxpayer-funded
-abortion-not-health-care-reform/john-boehner.

38. George H. W. Bush, *Speaking of Freedom: The Collected Speeches* (New York: Scribner, 2011), 5–15.

39. Jeffrey Birnbaum and Alan Murray, *Showdown at Gucci Gulch* (New York: Vintage Books, 1988), 160–73; quote on 166.

40. Jonathan Cohn, "How They Did It: The Inside Account of Health Care Reform's Triumph," *New Republic*, June 10, 2010, 14–25; quote on 25.

41. Representative Xavier Becerra (D-CA), former chairman of the Congressional Hispanic Caucus, quoted by Robert Pear and Jim Rutenberg, "Senators in Bipartisan Deal on Broad Immigration Bill," *New York Times*, May 17, 2007.

42. Senator Orrin Hatch (R-UT), *Congressional Record* 153 (June 28, 2007), S8661.

43. As Representative Ron Paul (R-TX) put it, "Supporters use very creative language to try and convince us that amnesty is not really amnesty, but when individuals who have entered the United States illegally are granted citizenship—regardless of the fees they are charged—what you have is amnesty…The much-vaunted Sonate "compromise" on immigration is a compromise all right: a compromise of our laws, a compromise of our sovereignty, and a compromise of the Second Amendment" ("Immigration 'Compromise' Sells Out Our Sovereignty," May 28, 2007, Congressman Ron Paul, http://paul.house.gov/index.php?option=com_content&task=view&id=1090&Itemid=69).

44. Dan Balz, "A Failure of Leadership in a Flawed Political Culture," *Washington Post*, June 8, 2007.

45. Ron Hutcheson and William Douglas, "Immigration Bill under Assault from Powerful Interest Groups," McClatchy Newspapers, May 27, 2007, http://www.mcclatchydc.com/2007/05/27/16491/immigration-bill-under-assault.html.

46. *Congressional Record* 153 (June 6, 2007), S7099.

47. Quoted in Carl Hulse, "Kennedy Plea Was Last Gasp for Immigration Bill," *New York Times*, June 9, 2007.

48. Carrie Budoff Brown, "Senate Immigration Compromise Collapses," *Politico*, June 8, 2007, http://dyn.politico.com/printstory.cfm?uuid=083C263E-3048-5C12-001103F31E2C3600.

49. Quoted in ibid.

50. They "raised objections, for example, when senators asked to dispense with further proceedings under a quorum call or to explain their reasons for opposing requests for unanimous consent" (Robert

Pear, "Proposals from Both Sides Fail in Immigration Debate," *New York Times*, June 28, 2007).

51. Quoted in ibid.

52. Brown, "Senate Immigration Compromise Collapses."

53. Quoted in ibid.

54. Balz, "A Failure of Leadership."

55. Quoted in ibid.

56. Senate Minority Leader Mitch McConnell, quoted by Jonathan Weisman, "Immigration Bill Dies in Senate," *Washington Post*, June 29, 2007.

57. Quoted in Hulse, "Kennedy Plea Was Last Gasp for Immigration Bill."

58. Ibid.

59. Ibid. (emphasis added).

CHAPTER 3: SEEKING COMPROMISE

1. Belinda Luscombe, "10 Questions for Alan Simpson," *Time*, August 8, 2011, 64.

2. Eyder Peralta, "Alan Simpson: If Lawmakers Can't Compromise, They Should 'Go Home,'" *The Two-Way: NPR's News Blog*, August 9, 2011, http://www.npr.org/blogs/thetwo-way/2011/08/09/ 139237356/alan-simpson-if-lawmakers-cant-compromise-they -should-go-home. Also note House Democratic Whip Steny Hoyer's plea during budget negotiations in the spring of 2011: "We are in a dangerous place when compromise—which is essentially the job description of a legislator in a free society—is enough to spark a revolt. For the rest of us—members of both parties who understand that legislating means compromising—it's time to find common ground and prevent a government shutdown." Representative Steny H. Hoyer (D-MD), "Whip Hoyer: It's Time to Cut and Compromise, Ensure Cuts We Agree On Do Not Undermine Americans' Shared Values," March 31, 2011, http://www.hoyer.house.gov/index.php?option=com_content &view=article&id=2742:hoyer-its-time-to-cut-and-compromise -ensure-cuts-we-agree-on-do-not-undermine-americans-shared -values-&catid=15:floor-statements&Itemid=84.

3. Quoted in Shailagh Murray, "Republicans Urge Democrats to Start All Over on Health Care," *Washington Post*, January 31, 2010, http://voices.washingtonpost.com/44/2010/01/republicans-urge -democrats-to.html?wprss=44.

4. Doris Kearns Goodwin, *Lyndon Johnson and the American Dream* (New York: St. Martin's Press, 1991), 154.

5. Hugh Davis Graham, "The Civil Rights Act of 1964," in *The Civil Rights Era: Origins and Development of National Policy, 1960–1972* (New York: Oxford University Press, 1990), 125–52; and Robert Dallek, *Flawed Giant: Lyndon Johnson and His Times, 1961–1973* (New York: Oxford University Press, 1999), 114, 120.

6. He described the "overall good" of the bill as dealing "with 12 million undocumented immigrants in a constructive way," by giving "them an opportunity to escape the fear they now have that they will be detected at any time," and by giving "us an opportunity to identify those who are not contributing, who have criminal records, who ought to be deported," and by better securing the border and establishing a more rigorous system of employer verification (*Congressional Record* 153 [June 6, 2007], S7099).

7. Mill did not present a full theory of compromise or even a systematic set of criteria. The list of considerations is drawn from his theoretical writings and based on his own statements and actions while serving in Parliament. See Dennis F. Thompson, "Mill in Parliament: When Should a Philosopher Compromise?," in *J. S. Mill's Political Thought*, ed. Nadia Urbinati and Alex Zakaras (Cambridge: Cambridge University Press, 2007), 166–99.

8. Frances Kamm, "The Philosopher as Insider and Outsider," *Journal of Medicine & Philosophy* 15, no. 4 (1990): 347–74; quote on 360.

9. Ibid.

10. See James Bohman, *Public Deliberation: Pluralism, Complexity, and Democracy* (Cambridge, MA: MIT Press, 1996), 89–104; quote on 91–92; and Henry Richardson, *Democratic Autonomy: Public Reasoning about the Ends of Policy* (Oxford: Oxford University Press, 2002), 144–61; quote on 146–47.

11. Quoted in Ben Smith, "Health Reform Foes Plan Obama's 'Waterloo,'" *Politico*, October 23, 2011, http://www.politico.com/blogs/bensmith/0709/Health_reform_foes_plan_Obamas_Waterloo.html.

12. Quoted in Ryan Lizza, "The Gatekeeper: Rahm Emanuel on the Job," *New Yorker*, March 2, 2009, 24.

13. Ibid.

14. Quoted in John F. Witte, "The Tax Reform Act of 1986: A New Era in Tax Politics?" *American Politics Research* 19, no. 4 (1991): 450, citing Jeffrey Birnbaum and Alan Murray, *Showdown at Gucci Gulch* (New York: Vintage Books, 1988), 19.

15. Bill Bradley, "Tax Reform's Lesson for Health Care Reform," *New York Times*, August 30, 2009.

16. For more on how what we call the suspension of motive cynicism may have worked, see Randall Strahan, "Members' Goals and Coalition-Building Strategies in the US House: The Case of Tax Reform," *Journal of Politics* 51, no. 2 (1989): 381; and Witte, "The Tax Reform Act of 1986," 447, 450.

17. Amy Gutmann and Dennis Thompson, *Democracy and Disagreement* (Cambridge, MA: Harvard University Press, 1996), 84–94; and Gutmann and Thompson, *Why Deliberative Democracy?* (Princeton, NJ: Princeton University Press, 2004), 7, 85–90, 92, 181–87.

18. Robert Pear, "Senate Approves Children's Health Bill," *New York Times*, January 29, 2009. An earlier bipartisan bill was vetoed by President Bush in 2001.

19. A recent survey of the literature on negotiation observes that "mutual trust [has been shown to be]...an essential ingredient in effective...negotiations" (Leigh Thompson, Jiunwen Wang, and Brian C. Gunia, "Negotiation," *Annual Review of Psychology* 61 [2010]: 501).

20. Senator Orrin Hatch, "Hatch Statement on the Passing of Senator Ted Kennedy," United States Senator Orrin Hatch, August 26, 2009, http://hatch.senate.gov/public/index.cfm/releases?ID=56fbf55f-1b78-be3e-e00e-6c461ee9373e.

21. Ronald Brownstein, *The Second Civil War: How Extreme Partisanship Has Paralyzed Washington and Polarized America* (New York: Penguin Press, 2008), 346.

22. Ibid., 248.

23. Ibid.

24. Ibid., 242.

25. Brendan Nyhan, "Why the 'Death Panel' Myth Wouldn't Die: Misinformation in the Health Care Reform Debate," *Forum* 8, no. 1, article 5 (2010), http://www.bepress.com/forum/vol8/iss1/art5; and Jonathan Alter, *The Promise: President Obama, Year One* (New York: Simon and Schuster, 2010), 257. On the other side, some liberal Democrats—"imitating tea-party conservatives"—turned on their party colleagues and proposed running TV ads "against foot-dragging moderates they considered DINOs ('Democrats in name only')" (idem, 407).

26. Quoted in Lisa Demer, "Murkowski: Don't Tell Lies about the Health-Care Reform Bill," *Anchorage Daily News*, August 12, 2009.

27. The legal scholar Cass Sunstein, chiefly discussing the Court, recommends a similar strategy in "Incompletely Theorized Agreements," *Harvard Law Review* 108, no. 7 (1995): 1733–72.

28. American Political Science Association, "Toward a More Responsible Two-Party System: A Report of the Committee on Political Parties," *American Political Science Review* 44, no. 3 (pt. 2, supplement) (1950): esp. 1–14.

29. Brownstein, *The Second Civil War*, 367.

30. Russell Muirhead, "Respectable Partisanship," in *The Arts of Rule*, ed. S. Krause and M. A. McGrail (Lanham, MD: Rowman & Littlefield, 2009), 392; Muirhead, "A Defense of Party Spirit," *Perspectives on Politics* 4, no. 4 (2006): 719; and Nancy Rosenblum, *On the Side of Angels: An Appreciation of Parties and Partisanship* (Princeton, NJ: Princeton University Press, 2008), 361–62. Also see Jonathan White and Lea Ypi, "On Partisan Political Justification," *American Political Science Review* 105, no. 2 (2011): 381–96.

31. Muirhead, "Respectable Partisanship," 392.

32. Rosenblum, *On the Side of Angels*, 361–62.

33. Ibid., 401–8. Also see Lisa Disch et al., "Parties, Partisanship, and Democratic Politics: Review Symposium for *On the Side of the Angels: An Appreciation of Parties and Partisanship*, by Nancy Rosenblum," *Perspectives on Politics* 7, no. 3 (2009): 621–29.

34. Rosenblum, *On the Side of Angels*, 402.

35. Brownstein, *The Second Civil War*, 342.

36. Ibid., 248.

37. Representative Jeff Flake (R-AZ), quoted by Brownstein, *The Second Civil War*, 248–49.

38. See Robert V. Remini, *The Edge of the Precipice: Henry Clay and the Compromise That Saved the Union* (New York: Basic Books, 2010); and David S. Heidler and Jeanne T. Heidler, *Henry Clay: The Essential American* (New York: Random House, 2010).

39. Remini, *Edge of the Precipice*, 158.

40. Peralta, "Alan Simpson."

41. See Susan Bibler Coutin, *Nation of Emigrants* (Ithaca, NY: Cornell University Press, 2007), 179. For a defense of the compromise by its coauthors, in light of the more recent failed attempt at immigration reform, see Romano L. Mazzoli and Alan K. Simpson, "Enacting Immigration Reform, Again," *Washington Post*, September 15, 2006, http://www.washingtonpost.com/wp-dyn/content/article/2006/09/14/AR2006091401179.html.

42. Wayne Cornelius, Philip L. Martin, and James Frank Hollifield, *Controlling Immigration: A Global Perspective* (Stanford, CA: Stanford University Press, 1994), 67.

43. Hendrick Hertzberg, "The Book on Barack," *New Yorker*, October 3, 2011, 22.

44. The final version of the bill is called the Tax Relief, Unemployment Insurance Reauthorization, and Job Creation Act of 2010, Public Law 111-312, 111th Cong., http://www.gpo.gov/fdsys/pkg/BILLS-111hr4853enr/pdf/BILLS-111hr4853enr.pdf. The House voted 277–148, with 139 Democrats and 138 Republicans voting in favor, and 112 Democrats and 36 Republicans voting against. The Senate bill passed with strong bipartisan support, 81–19.

45. Peter Baker, "In Deal with G.O.P., Portent for Next 2 Years," *New York Times*, December 6, 2010.

46. Dan Friedman, "GOP Will Filibuster All Bills if Taxes, Budget Not Addressed," *National Journal*, December 1, 2010, http://www.nationaljournal.com/congress/gop-will-filibuster-all-bills-if-taxes-budget-not-addressed-20101201.

47. CNN Wire Staff, "Democratic Procedural Votes on Extending Bush Tax Cuts Fail in Senate," CNN Politics, December 4, 2010, http://articles.cnn.com/2010-12-04/politics/senate.tax.vote_1_tax-cuts-george-w-bush-era-tax-end-debate?_s=PM:POLITICS.

48. Christina Bellantoni, "Tax Cut Tussle: House Democrats Split on Whether to Hold Vote," *Talking Points Memo*, September 13, 2010, http://tpmdc.talkingpointsmemo.com/2010/09/tax-cut-tussle-house-democrats-split-on-whether-to-hold-vote.php.

49. CBS News, *Face the Nation*, "September 12, 2010: Transcript," http://www.cbsnews.com/htdocs/pdf/FTN_091210.pdf. However, some saw Boehner's comment as a purely political tactic: "[H]e was attempting to rob Democrats of a potent campaign line—that the GOP is holding middle-class tax cuts hostage to breaks for the very wealthy" (Shailagh Murray and Lori Montgomery, "Republicans Say They'll Push to Extend Tax Cuts," *Washington Post*, September 13, 2010). For another example, see "CNBC's Larry Kudlow Speaks with Senator Mitch McConnell Today on CNBC's 'The Kudlow Report,'" September 15, 2010, http://www.cnbc.com/id/39077006/Cnbc_Transcript_Cnbc_S_Larry_Kudlow_Speaks_With_Senator_Mitch_Mcconnell_Today_On_Cnbc_S_The_Kudlow_Report.

50. Quoted in David M. Herszenhorn and Sheryl Gay Stolberg, "Obama Defends Tax Deal, but His Party Stays Hostile," *New York Times*, December 7, 2010; and Michael Shear and Jackie Calmes, "Biden Tries, Again, to Sell Tax Compromise to Hill Democrats," *New York Times Blogs*, December 8, 2010, http://thecaucus.blogs.nytimes.com/2010/12/08/biden-tries-again-to-sell-tax-compromise-to-hill-democrats.

51. White House, Office of the Press Secretary, "Press Conference by the President," December 7, 2010, http://m.whitehouse.gov/the-press-office/2010/12/07/press-conference-president.

52. Carl Hulse and Jackie Calmes, "Biden and G.O.P. Leader Helped Hammer Out Bipartisan Tax Accord," *New York Times*, December 7, 2010.

53. Ibid.

54. Quoted in Matt Bai, "Is 'Triangulation' Just Another Word for the Politics of the Possible?," *New York Times*, December 16, 2010.

55. Hulse and Calmes, "Biden and G.O.P. Leader Helped Hammer Out Bipartisan Tax Accord."

56. David Leonhardt, "In Tax Plan, a Boost for Jobs," *New York Times*, December 7, 2010.

57. Charles Krauthammer, "Swindle of the Year," *Washington Post,* December 10, 2010.

58. "The President Surrenders," the headline of a prominent column, captured the mood of much of the liberal wing of the party (Paul Krugman, *New York Times*, August 1, 2011). Anticipating the result, Senator Robert Menendez (D-NJ) said it was "not fair, and I will not support it" (*New York Times*, August 2, 2011). Shortly after the deal was announced, Louisiana Governor Bobby Jindal, speaking to the Republican National Committee, called it simply "a mistake," and received a standing ovation ("Bobby Jindal Criticizes Debt 'Compromise,'" *Politico*, August 4, 2011, http://www.politico.com/news/stories/0811/60688.html). All but one of the candidates competing for the Republican nomination for president declared themselves opposed to the compromise.

59. Fareed Zakaria, "The Debt Deal's Failure," *Time*, August 15, 2011, 30–33.

60. See Binyamin Appelbaum and Helene Cooper, "White House Debates Fight on Economy," *New York Times*, August 14, 2011.

CHAPTER 4: CAMPAIGNING V. GOVERNING

1. The quotes and comments are adapted from Obama's statements and speeches during the campaign. See, e.g., Tomás Alberto Ávila, ed., *Barack Obama: Campaign Speeches* (Providence, RI: Milenio Publishing, 2008). On the dispute with Hillary Clinton about the individual mandate, see Lori Robertson et al., "Clinton vs. Obama: Who's Right on Health Care, Social Security?" FactCheck.org, November 16, 2007, http://www.factcheck.org/clinton_vs_obama.html.

2. Quoted in Jonathan Alter, *The Promise: President Obama, Year One* (New York: Simon and Schuster, 2010), 249.

3. "Kerry Discusses $87 Billion Comment," CNN Politics, September 30, 2004, http://articles.cnn.com/2004-09-30/politics/kerry

.comment_1_kerry-campaign-spokesman-inarticulate-moments
-bush-campaign?_s=PM:ALLPOLITICS.

4. "Bush Ad Twists Kerry's Words on Iraq," FactCheck.org, September 27, 2004, http://www.factcheck.org/bush_ad_twists_kerrys
_words_on_iraq.html.

5. Jeff Zeleny and Jim Rutenberg, "Obama Retools 2008 Machine
for Tough Run," *New York Times,* June 5, 2011.

6. See, e.g., Ronald A. Faucheux, ed., *Winning Elections: Political
Campaign Management, Strategy and Tactics* (Lanham, MD: Rowman and Littlefield, 2003), 67–68.

7. Gary C. Jacobson, *The Politics of Congressional Elections*, 7th
ed. (New York: Longman, 2009), 63; and Martin P. Wattenberg, *The
Rise of Candidate-Centered Politics: Presidential Elections of the
1980s* (Cambridge, MA: Harvard University Press, 1992).

8. Morris P. Fiorina, with Samuel J. Abrams, *Disconnect: The
Breakdown of Representation in American Politics* (Norman: University of Oklahoma Press, 2009), 57.

9. Paul S. Herrnson, *Congressional Elections*, 5th ed. (Washington, DC: Congressional Quarterly Press, 2008), 205.

10. Thomas M. Holbrook and Scott D. McClurg, "The Mobilization of Core Supporters: Campaigns, Turnout, and Electoral Composition in United States Presidential Elections," *American Journal of
Political Science* 49 (2005): 689–701; and James A. Gardner, *What
Are Campaigns For?* (New York: Oxford University Press, 2009),
148–49.

11. For surveys of the literature (with references), see Gardner,
What Are Campaigns For?, 83–113; Michael Alvarez, *Information
and Elections* (Ann Arbor: University of Michigan Press, 1997); and
Thomas M. Holbrook, *Do Campaigns Matter?* (Thousand Oaks, CA:
Sage Publications, 1996). Also see Richard Johnston, Michael G.
Hagen, and Kathleen Hall Jamieson, *The 2000 Presidential Election
and the Foundations of Party Politics* (Cambridge: Cambridge University Press, 2004); David M. Farrell and Rüdiger Schmitt-Beck, *Do
Political Campaigns Matter?* (New York: Routledge, 2002); Shanto
Iyengar and Adam F. Simon, "New Perspectives and Evidence on
Political Communication and Campaign Effects," *Annual Review of
Psychology* 51 (2000): 149–69; and Andrew Gelman and Gary King,
"Why Are American Presidential Election Polls So Variable When
Votes Are So Predictable?," *American Political Science Review* 23
(1993): 419–51.

12. See especially Johnston et al., *The 2000 Presidential Election
and the Foundations of Party Politics*, 4, 60–64, 174–75.

13. For comprehensive surveys and analyses, see Richard R. Lau, Lee Sigelman, Caroline Heldman, and Paul Babbitt, "The Effects of Negative Political Advertisements: A Meta-Analytic Assessment," *American Political Science Review* 93 (1999): 851–75; and Richard R. Lau and Ivy Brown Rovner, "Negative Campaigning," *Annual Review of Political Science* 12 (2009): 285–306. Also see Larry M. Bartels, "Campaign Quality: Standards for Evaluation, Benchmarks for Reform," in *Campaign Reform: Insights and Evidence*, ed. Larry M. Bartels and Lynn Vavreck (Ann Arbor: University of Michigan Press, 2000), 10–13. But see Richard R. Lau and Gerald M. Pomper, "Effectiveness of Negative Campaigning in U.S. Senate Elections," *American Journal of Political Science* 46 (2002): 47–66.

14. Lynn Vavreck, "How Does It All 'Turnout'? Exposure to Attack Advertising, Campaign Interest, and Participation in American Presidential Elections," in *Campaign Reform*, 99–100; John G. Geer, "Assessing Attack Advertising: A Silver Lining," in *Campaign Reform*, 62–78; and Kathleen Hall Jamieson, *Everything You Think You Know about Politics ... And Why You're Wrong* (New York: Basic Books, 2000), 97–114.

15. Geer, "Assessing Attack Advertising"; and Jamieson, *Everything You Think You Know about Politics*.

16. See Amy Gutmann and Dennis Thompson, *Democracy and Disagreement* (Cambridge, MA: Harvard University Press, 1996), 358–60.

17. Joseph Schumpeter, *Capitalism, Socialism and Democracy* (London: George Allen and Unwin, 1961), 269.

18. For a critique, see Gerry Mackie, "Schumpeter's Leadership Democracy," *Political Theory* 37, no. 1 (2009): 128–53. For a partial defense, see Jeffrey Edward Green, "Three Theses on Schumpeter: Response to Mackie," *Political Theory* 38, no. 2 (2010): 268–75.

19. Schumpeter, *Capitalism, Socialism and Democracy*, 295.

20. Ibid., 263–64, 295.

21. Ibid., 271. Everyone is free to compete for office but only "in the same sense in which everyone is free to start another textile mill" (272).

22. Ibid., 271.

23. Ian Shapiro, *The State of Democratic Theory* (Princeton, NJ: Princeton University Press, 2003), 58–62, 108–9. Also see Alan I. Abramowitz, *The Disappearing Center: Engaged Citizens, Polarization, and American Democracy* (New Haven, CT: Yale University Press, 2010), 1–14, 158–72.

24. Shapiro, *The State of Democratic Theory*, 57.

25. Ibid., 59–62.

26. Ibid., 60.

27. Ibid., 60–61. Bipartisan gerrymandering is cited as a prime example of "anticompetitive collusion in restraint of democracy." However, the evidence for the negative effects of congressional redistricting is mixed (see the studies cited below: page 247, note 45). Furthermore, insofar as gerrymandering reduces competition, any democratic theory that recognizes the value of competitive elections can criticize the practice and can do so without elevating either competition or compromise to a first principle. Notice also that deliberative democrats can object to politicians' making decisions about redistricting whether or not the result weakens competition. Representatives should not have the power to choose whom they will represent. The typical process of redistricting is "not one in which the people select their representatives, but in which the representatives have selected the people" (Vera v. Richards, 861 F Supp. 1304, 1334 [S.D. Tex. 1994]).

28. Gutmann and Thompson, *Democracy and Disagreement*; and idem, *Why Deliberative Democracy?* (Princeton, NJ: Princeton University Press, 2004).

29. Norman Ornstein and Thomas Mann, eds., *The Permanent Campaign and Its Future* (Washington, DC: American Enterprise Institute, 2000). Also see the references listed in the Introduction, page 219, note 1.

30. For a sharp contrast between the concepts of campaigning and governing, see Hugh Heclo, "Campaigning and Governing: A Conspectus," in *The Permanent Campaign*, 4–15. Heclo posits three differences: campaigning is focused on a single decision point in time, whereas governing involves many interconnected points of outcome through time; campaigning is adversarial whereas governing is collaborative; and campaigning is an exercise in persuasion whereas governing requires deliberation.

31. The permanent campaign damages the democratic process in other ways as well—for example, the increase in public cynicism and disengagement. But these effects have received more attention than the damage to the capacity for compromise (see Ornstein and Mann, *The Permanent Campaign*, 224–30).

32. Quoted in Peter Baker and Carl Hulse, "Off Script, Obama and the G.O.P. Vent Politely," *New York Times*, January 30, 2010.

33. Trip Gabriel, "Election Cycle Emerges as the Year of the Pledge, but Some Candidates Resist," *New York Times*, July 17, 2011. Also see the editorial, "Signing Away the Right to Govern," *New York Times*, July 19, 2011.

34. Donna R. Hoffman, quoted in Gabriel, "Election Cycle Emerges as the Year of the Pledge."

35. Major Garrett, "Top GOP Priority: Make Obama a One-Term President," *National Journal,* October 23, 2010.

36. David Brady and Morris Fiorina, "Congress in the Era of the Permanent Campaign," in *The Permanent Campaign,* 134–61.

37. Fritz Plasser and Gunder Plasser, *Global Political Campaigning* (Westport, CT: Praeger, 2002), 15–106, 343–52; and Jay G. Blumler and Michael Gurevitch, "'Americanization' Reconsidered: U.K.–U.S. Campaign Communications across Time," in *Mediated Politics,* ed. W. Lance Bennett and Robert M. Entman (Cambridge: Cambridge University Press, 2001), 380–403.

38. Heclo, "Campaigning and Governing: A Conspectus," 19–29.

CHAPTER 5: GOVERNING WITH CAMPAIGNING

1. Senator Mark Udall, "Udall Urges Congress to Put Aside Partisan Divisions—Sit Together during State of the Union," January 12, 2011, http://markudall.senate.gov/?p=press_release&id=877.

2. Jim Cooper, "Fixing Congress," *Boston Review* (May/June 2011): 12–34.

3. Cass Sunstein, *Going to Extremes: How Like Minds Unite and Divide* (New York: Oxford University Press, 2011).

4. Norman J. Ornstein, "Ending the Permanent Campaign," *Boston Review* (May/June 2011): 20–21. Also see Thomas E. Mann and Norman J. Ornstein, *The Broken Branch: How Congress Is Failing America and How to Get It Back on Track* (New York: Oxford University Press, 2008), 232–33.

5. David E. Price, "The Advantages and Disadvantages of Partisanship," *Boston Review* (May/June 2011): 27–30.

6. Norman Ornstein and Thomas Mann, eds., *The Permanent Campaign and Its Future* (Washington, DC: American Enterprise Institute, 2000), 229.

7. Robert A. Dahl, *Polyarchy: Participation and Opposition* (New Haven, CT: Yale University Press, 1972).

8. On the filibuster, see Gregory J. Wawro and Eric Schickler, *Filibuster: Obstruction and Lawmaking in the United States Senate* (Princeton, NJ: Princeton University Press, 2006); Sarah A. Binder and Steven S. Smith, *Politics or Principle? Filibustering in the United States Senate* (Washington, DC: Brookings Institution Press, 1997); and Gregory J. Wawro and Eric Schickler, "Legislative Obstructionism," *Annual Review of Political Science* 13 (2010): 297–319.

9. Barbara Sinclair, "The New World of U.S. Senators," in *Congress Reconsidered*, ed. Lawrence C. Dodd and Bruce I. Oppenheimer, 9th ed. (Washington, DC: Congressional Quarterly Press, 2008), 11.

10. For an analysis of the episode, see Sarah A. Binder, Anthony J. Madonna, and Steven S. Smith, "Going Nuclear, Senate Style," *Perspectives on Politics* 5, no. 4 (2007): 729–40.

11. Wawro and Schickler, "Legislative Obstructionism," 308.

12. Binder et al. argue that "the minority came out better than the majority" ("Going Nuclear," 737). Wawro and Schickler reach the opposite conclusion ("Legislative Obstructionism," 308).

13. The cloture procedure is also sometimes used by the majority for its own electoral advantage. It can enable the majority to block nongermane amendments, which under normal (noncloture) proceedings are permitted and sometimes are used to force senators to take a position that could be used against them in the next election. Matthew S. Urdan, "Filibuster," in *Congress A to Z*, ed. David R. Tarr and Ann O'Connor, 4th ed. (Washington, DC: CQ Press, 2003).

14. See Binder and Smith: "There is little theoretical basis or sustained empirical support for the proposition that supermajority requirements produce policy outcomes more likely to reflect the interests of congressional and popular majorities" (*Politics or Principle*, 203).

15. Wawro and Schickler, "Legislative Obstructionism," 315.

16. On the dispute about these alternative explanations, see Wawro and Schickler, "Legislative Obstructionism," 314.

17. Alexis de Tocqueville, *Democracy in America*, trans. Jacob Peter Mayer (New York: Harper and Row, 1969), 119.

18. Kathryn Dunn Tenpas, "Institutionalized Politics: The White House Office of Political Affairs," *Presidential Studies Quarterly* 26, no. 2 (Spring 1996): 511.

19. United States, Office of Special Counsel, *Investigation of Political Activities by White House and Federal Agency Officials during the 2006 Midterm Elections* (Washington, DC: U.S. Office of Special Counsel, 2011).

20. Ibid., 18.

21. Richard W. Painter, *Getting the Government America Deserves: How Ethics Reform Can Make a Difference* (New York: Oxford University Press, 2009), 245–53.

22. Josh Gerstein and Matt Negrin, "W.H. Releases DNC Meet Names," *Politico*, June 24, 2011, http://www.politico.com/news/stories/0611/57745.html.

23. *The Congressional Globe*, 25th Cong., 3d Sess., app. 409 (1839) (statement of Sen. Rives).

24. Aristotle, *Politics*, bk. 6, chap. 2, 1317b, in *Complete Works of Aristotle*, ed. Jonathan Barnes (Princeton, NJ: Princeton University Press, 1985), 2:2091. For a contemporary analysis of the popular and academic arguments (from the perspective of a proponent), see Einer Elhauge, "Are Term Limits Undemocratic?" *University of Chicago Law Review* 64 (Winter 1997): 83–203. More generally, see Karl T. Kurtz, Bruce E. Cain, and Richard G. Niemi, *Institutional Change in American Politics: The Case of Term Limits* (Ann Arbor: University of Michigan Press, 2007); and Marjorie Sarbaugh-Thompson, Charles D. Elder, Richard Elling, and John Strate, *The Political and Institutional Effects of Term Limits* (New York: Palgrave Macmillan, 2006).

25. The quotations come from one of the most prominent pieces of legislation in the movement in the states in the 1990s to establish term limits: "Term Limitation Amendment," adopted November 3, 1992, Arkansas Constitution, amendment 73, sec. 1–3 (sec. 3 superseded by amendment 76). It was the subject of the leading Supreme Court case on term limits, U.S. Term Limits, Inc. v. Thornton, 514 U.S. 779 (1995), which struck down the congressional term limits but allowed the state limits to survive.

26. Sarbaugh-Thompson et al., *Political and Institutional Effects of Term Limits*, 120–22, 189.

27. Ibid., 196.

28. Anthony King, *Running Scared: Why America's Politicians Campaign Too Much and Govern Too Little* (New York: Routledge, 1997), 180–81; and Larry J. Sabato, *A More Perfect Constitution: 23 Proposals to Revitalize Our Constitution and Make America a Fairer Country* (New York: Walker and Co., 2007), 93–96.

29. King, *Running Scared*, 180.

30. James Madison, *Records of the Federal Convention of 1787*, ed. Max Farrand, rev. ed. (New Haven, CT: Yale University Press, 1966), 214–15 (entry for June 12). Also see James Madison, Federalist No. 63, in *The Federalist*, ed. Jacob E. Cooke (Middletown, CT: Wesleyan University Press, 1961), 423–24.

31. Madison, *Records*, 214. By the 1880s, the adverse effects of campaigning had become a salient argument for longer terms. Wisconsin Representative Thad C. Pound defended his proposed constitutional amendment extending the House term to three years mainly by arguing that it would make "attendant evils" of elections "less frequent"—the "embittered wranglings, business disturbances,

and corrupting influences" ("Congressman Pound. His Own Idea of
His Bill to Lengthen the Terms of the President and the Representatives in Congress," *New York Times*, January 2, 1880, http://query
.nytimes.com/mem/archive-free/pdf?res=F00A12FB3A551B7A93C
0A9178AD85F448884F9).

32. David M. Herszenhorn, "Two Missed Moment to Solemnly
Swear," *New York Times Blogs*, January 6, 2011, http://thecaucus
.blogs.nytimes.com/2011/01/06/two-missed-moment-to-solemnly-swear.

33. Columnist Gail Collins wrote: "The lawmakers, Pete Sessions
of Texas and Mike Fitzpatrick of Pennsylvania, did raise their hands
and recite the oath of office in front of the televised version of the
event. But really, what if we'd all done that? If I'd known it was an
option, I would definitely have sworn myself in and then gotten my
picture taken with John Boehner" ("God Save the Debate," *New York
Times*, January 8, 2011).

34. Mark C. Alexander, "Let Them Do Their Jobs: The Compelling Government Interest in Protecting the Time of Candidates and
Elected Officials," *Loyola University of Chicago Law Journal* 37
(2005): 674.

35. Dennis F. Thompson, *Just Elections* (Chicago: University of
Chicago Press, 2002), 105–18.

36. Alexander, "Let Them Do Their Jobs," 669–772; Justin Kramer,
"Randall v. Sorrell: A New Wrinkle in the Campaign Finance Reform
Debate," *St. John's Journal of Legal Commentary* 22, no. 1 (2007):
261–94. The earliest (and for a long time the only) sustained dis-
cussion of the time-protection argument is found in Vincent Blasi,
"Free Speech and the Widening Gyre of Fund-Raising: Why Cam-
paign Spending Limits May Not Violate the First Amendment after
All," *Columbia Law Review* 94, no. 4 (1994): 1281–1325.

37. Randall v. Sorrell, 548 U.S. 230 (2006), 278–79. Justice Stevens here cites Alexander, "Let Them Do Their Jobs."

38. See Anthony Corrado, Daniel R. Ortiz, Thomas E. Mann, and
Trevor Potter, eds., *The New Campaign Finance Sourcebook* (Wash-
ington, DC: Brookings Institution Press, 2005); and the Campaign
Finance Institute, http://www.cfinst.org/about.aspx.

39. In the most recent case involving expenditure limits, only
three members of the Court were willing to consider upholding
the limits set in Vermont's reform (Randall v. Sorrell, 548 U.S. 230
[2006]). For criticism of the view that the principle of free speech is
violated by restrictions on expenditures, see John Rawls, *Political
Liberalism* (New York: Columbia University Press, 1993), 326–27,
359–63. Also see Ronald Dworkin, *Sovereign Virtue: The Theory*

and Practice of Equality (Cambridge, MA: Harvard University Press, 2002), chap. 10; and David A. Strauss, "Corruption, Equality, and Campaign Finance Reform," *Columbia Law Review* 94 (May 1994): 1369–89.

40. See Costas Panagopoulos, ed., *Public Financing in American Elections* (Philadelphia: Temple University Press, 2011).

41. The most important recent initiative for grassroots funding of campaigns is the Fair Elections Now Act (S. 750 and H.R. 1404), reintroduced in 2011 in the Senate by Dick Durbin (D-IL) and in the House by John Larson (D-CT), Walter Jones Jr. (R-NC), and Chellie Pingree (D-ME). The bill gives congressional candidates the option of receiving public funding if they raise a large number of donations of $100 or less from in-state donors, and additional public funds if they continue to raise small donations in their state. The cost for Senate races would be covered by a small fee on large government contractors; for House races, it would come from a small portion of revenues generated through the auction of unused broadcast spectrum. S.750. IS—Fair Elections Now Act, 112th Congress (2011–2012), http://thomas.loc.gov/cgi-bin/query/z?c112:s750.is:; and H.R.1404.IH—Fair Elections Now, Act 112th Congress (2011–2012) http://thomas.loc.gov/cgi-bin/query/z?c112:h1404.ih.

42. Mann and Ornstein, *The Broken Branch*, 237.

43. Ibid.

44. Ibid., 237–38.

45. It is often suggested that one way to encourage politicians who are more inclined to compromise is to try to rein in partisan gerrymandering, which is assumed to contribute to polarization by making districts more homogenous and successful candidates more extreme. But as we have indicated, reducing polarization is not necessary for encouraging compromise (though it may help). Furthermore, the assumption that gerrymandering produces polarization is not well supported by the evidence (Nolan McCarty, Keith T. Poole, and Howard Rosenthal, "Does Gerrymandering Cause Polarization?," *American Journal of Political Science* 53, no. 3 [2009]: 666–80). Nor does the redistricting process protect incumbents, as is often assumed (Stephen Ansolabehere and James M. Snyder, *The End of Inequality: One Person, One Vote and the Transformation of American Politics* [New York: Norton, 2008], 262–71). There are good reasons to reform the redistricting process, but promoting compromise is not one of them. See Dennis F. Thompson, "Election Time: Normative Implications of Temporal Properties of the Electoral Process in the United States," *American Political Science Review* 98, no. 1 (2004): 52–56.

On redistricting generally, see Thomas E. Mann and Bruce E. Cain, eds., *Party Lines: Competition, Partisanship, and Congressional Redistricting* (Washington, DC: Brookings Institution Press, 2005).

46. Elisabeth R. Gerber, "Strategic Voting and Candidate Policy Positions," in *Voting at the Political Fault Line: California's Experiment with the Blanket Primary*, ed. Bruce E. Cain and Elisabeth R. Gerber (Berkeley: University of California Press, 2002), 192–213.

47. See, generally, Cain and Gerber, *Voting at the Political Fault Line*.

48. California Democratic Party v. Jones, 530 U.S. 567, 568 (2000).

49. Washington State Grange v. Washington State Republican Party, 128 S. Ct. 1184 (2008).

50. For a fuller assessment from the perspective of democratic theory, see Thompson, *Just Elections*, 80–87.

51. Elisabeth R. Gerber, "Strategic Voting and Candidate Policy Positions," 192–213.

52. California Democratic Party v. Jones, 169 F. 3d at 658.

53. Voter registration and voting day reforms in the United States to date have been quite limited, and (perhaps as a consequence) have not done nearly as much as their advocates expected by way of increasing turnout. For an informative summary of the evidence, see Marjorie Randon Hershey, "What We Know about Voter-ID Laws, Registration, and Turnout," *PS* (January 2009): 87–91. Also see Michael J. Hammer, *Discount Voting: Voter Registration Reforms and Their Effects* (Cambridge: Cambridge University Press, 2009).

54. For evidence that more demanding forms of political engagement in the United States correlate with features of what we call the uncompromising mindset, see Diana C. Mutz, *Hearing the Other Side: Deliberative versus Participatory Democracy* (New York: Cambridge University Press, 2006).

55. Ibid., 125–51.

56. Morris P. Fiorina, with Samuel J. Abrams, *Disconnect: The Breakdown of Representation in American Politics* (Norman: University of Oklahoma Press, 2009), 87.

57. This summarizes the outlook, which we discussed in the introduction, of Alan I. Abramowitz, *The Disappearing Center: Engaged Citizens, Polarization, and American Democracy* (New Haven, CT: Yale University Press, 2010).

58. On citizens' assemblies, see Mark E. Warren and Hilary Pearse, eds., *Designing Deliberative Democracy: The British Columbia Citizens' Assembly* (Cambridge: Cambridge University Press, 2008), 20–49.

59. *Daily Show with Jon Stewart*, "Rally to Restore Sanity Announcement," September 16, 2010, http://www.thedailyshow.com/watch/thu-september-16-2010/rally-to-restore-sanity; and Jason Horowitz, Monica Hesse, and Dan Zak, "Jon Stewart, Stephen Colbert Host Rally to Restore Sanity and/or Fear on Mall," *Washington Post*, October 31, 2010.

60. "At a news conference after the rally, reporters asked Stewart what message he had sent to his constituency. 'We don't have a constituency,' he insisted" (Horowitz et al., "Jon Stewart, Stephen Colbert Host Rally to Restore Sanity").

61. Mutz, *Hearing the Other Side*, 147–51.

62. Mann and Ornstein conclude their wide-ranging critique and review of recommendations for reform thus: "Major change within Congress is most likely to originate outside Congress" (*Broken Branch*, 244).

63. Madison, *Records of the Federal Convention*, 2:249–50 (entry for August 10).

64. In a major study of this shift, Joseph N. Cappella and Kathleen Hall Jamieson write that "the Seventies and Eighties were a time of fundamental change in the distribution of media coverage from issue-based stories to ones that emphasize who is ahead and behind, and the strategies and tactics of campaigning necessary to position a candidate to get ahead or stay ahead" (*Spiral of Cynicism: The Press and the Public Good* [New York: Oxford University Press, 1997], 33). Also see Shanto Iyengar, "The Media Game: New Moves, Old Strategies," The Forum 9, no. 1 (2011): 1–6, http://pcl.stanford.edu/research/2011/iyengar-mediagame.pdf. For distinctions among types of horse race coverage and an argument that some types may be valuable, see Dennis F. Thompson, "The Primary Purpose of Presidential Primaries," *Political Science Quarterly* 125, no. 2 (2010): 226–29.

65. Cappella and Jamieson, *Spiral of Cynicism*, esp. 34–48.

66. Ibid., 48. Also see Iyengar, "The Media Game," 3; and Thomas Patterson, *Out of Order* (New York: Knopf, 1993).

67. Hugh Heclo, "Campaigning and Governing: A Conspectus" in *The Permanent Campaign,* 22. For evidence that horse race stories attract large audiences, see S. Iyengar, H. Norpoth, and K. Hahn, "Consumer Demand for Election News: The Horserace Sells," *Journal of Politics* 66 (2004): 157–75.

68. Cappella and Jamieson, *Spiral of Cynicism*, 17–35.

69. This is the overarching thesis of Cappella and Jamieson in *Spiral of Cynicism*. They usefully distinguish cynicism from skepticism about politics, the latter of which is a disposition to question

and to remain dubious about assertions made in politics until they are proven (ibid., 25–26).

70. Pew Research Center for the People and the Press, "Ideological News Sources: Who Watches and Why, Americans Spending More Time Following the News," September 12, 2010, 13–27, http://www.people-press.org/2010/09/12/section-1-watching-reading-and-listening-to-the-news.

71. See Marcus Prior, *Post-Broadcast Democracy: How Media Choice Increases Inequality in Political Involvement and Polarizes Elections* (New York: Cambridge University Press, 2007), 271–75; and Cass R. Sunstein, *Republic.com* (Princeton, NJ: Princeton University Press, 2001). But see Matthew Gentzkow and Jesse M. Shapiro, "Ideological Segregation Online and Offline," *Quarterly Journal of Economics* (November 3, 2011): 1–41, http://qje.oxford-journals.org/content/early/2011/11/03/qje.qjr044.full#abstract-1.

72. According to a recent Pew Research Center survey, among all the sources of the news today, "television stands apart not only because more people get news there, but also because people continue to spend more time getting news there than any other source" ("Ideological News Sources: Who Watches and Why, Americans Spending More Time Following the News," 17).

73. Pew Research Center, "Ideological News Sources," 2.

74. Ibid., 17, 28, 44.

75. Fact checking does not impress everyone, as can be seen in the websites that ignore the findings of FactCheck.org, and in some cases denounce it as "completely worthless." But looking at most of these sites, one gets the impression that they do not care much about facts, quite apart from fact checking. For example, Citizens Against ProObama Media Bias claims that FactCheck.org is intentionally deceiving the public about the existence of President Obama's Hawaiian birth certificate (http://citizensagainstproobamamediabias.wordpress.com).

76. Prior, *Post-Broadcast Democracy*, 271.

77. Larry M. Bartels, "Campaign Reform: Insights and Evidence," Report of the Task Force on Campaign Reform, in *Campaign Reform: Insights and Evidence*, ed. Larry M. Bartels and Lynn Vavreck (Ann Arbor: University of Michigan Press, 2000), 212–26, 231–35.

78. Marion R. Just, Ann N. Crigler, Dean E. Alger, and Timothy E. Cook, *Crosstalk: Citizens, Candidates, and the Media in a Presidential Campaign* (Chicago: University of Chicago Press, 1996), cited in Bartels, "Campaign Reform," 219, 241.

79. See Carnegie Corporation of New York, "The Future of Journalism Education," http://carnegie.org/programs/future-of-journalism -education.

80. Bartels, "Campaign Reform," 216–17.

81. Pulitzer Prizes, "Explanatory Reporting," http://www.pulitzer .org/bycat/Explanatory-Reporting.

82. Bruce Ackerman, *The Decline and Fall of the American Republic* (Cambridge, MA: Harvard University Press, 2010), 133–35.

83. Robert McChesney and John Nichols, *The Death and Life of American Journalism* (New York: Nation Books, 2010), 200–206.

84. Iyengar, "The Media Game," 3.

85. The Obama campaign, for example, posted on YouTube the complete video of his prime-time speech on race relations after the Reverend Jeremiah Wright controversy erupted. "It was immediately viewed by more than a million people. By the end of the campaign, 7 million people had watched the entire speech online" (Iyengar, "The Media Game," 5). Also see Steven Hill, "World Wide Webbed: The Obama Campaign's Masterful Use of the Internet," *Social Europe Journal* 4, no. 2 (2009): 9–15.

86. Prior, *Post-Broadcast Democracy*, 281–88. Also see James G. Webster, "Beneath the Veneer of Fragmentation: Television Audience Polarization in a Multichannel World," *Journal of Communication* 55, no. 2 (June 2005): 366–82.

87. One obstacle is that the political polarization reappears in the disagreements about the purposes of civic education: "Republicans are more likely to see teaching facts, respect for the military, and love of country as critical, while Democrats attach more importance to teaching values like tolerance" (Daniel K. Lautzenheiser, Andrew P. Kelly, and Cheryl Miller, *Contested Curriculum: How Teachers and Citizens View Civics Education*, AEI Program on American Citizenship, Policy Brief 1, [Washington, DC: American Enterprise Institute, 2011]).

88. Mutz, *Hearing the Other Side*, 150.

89. Bill Bishop, *The Big Sort: Why the Clustering of Like-Minded America Is Tearing Us Apart* (Boston: Houghton Mifflin, 2008).

90. See Diana E. Hess, *Controversy in the Classroom: The Democratic Power of Discussion* (New York: Routledge, 2009).

91. Ibid., 53–76.

92. Carnegie Corporation of New York and CIRCLE: The Center for Information and Research on Civic Learning and Engagement, *The Civic Mission of Schools* (New York: Carnegie Corporation, 2003), 6.

93. Hess, *Controversy in the Classroom*, 28. For a careful assessment of how teachers can make this kind of civic education effective, depending on the ideological homogeneity of their classroom setting, see Paula McAvoy and Diana Hess, "The Ethics of Political Disclosure in High School Classrooms," paper delivered at the American Political Science Association Annual Meeting, 2011.

94. For the tension between curricula that promote discussion in which students reason together and change their views, and curricula that encourage students to bring settled views to class and argue effectively for them, see Walter C. Parker, "Feel Free to Change Your Mind," Democracy & Education, 19, no. 2 (2011): article 9, http://democracyeducationjournal.org/home/vol19/iss2/9. Although these aims are not mutually exclusive, other studies have shown that the emphasis on one goal (such as participatory citizenship) can detract from the achievement of other goals (such as critical judgment about social justice). See Joel Westheimer and Joseph Kahne, "What Kind of Citizen? The Politics of Educating for Democracy," *American Educational Research Journal* 41, no. 2 (Summer 2004): 237–69.

95. A major national initiative in this spirit is Project Citizen, in which groups of students identify a problem in their community, explore alternative solutions, and agree on a policy to deal with it. Some critics of the project worry that the agreement may be forced, encouraging conformity and suppressing dissent. But the proponents of the project claim that under the right conditions the students learn not only how to deal with real problems but also how to compromise in the face of political disagreement. See Center for Civic Education and National Conference of State Legislatures, *Project Citizen: A Portfolio-Based Civic Education Program* (Washington, DC, 2008), http://www.civiced.org/pdfs/brochures/2008BchrProjCtznLR.pdf.

CONCLUSION

1. Peter Baker, "Hip, Hip—if Not Hooray—for a Standstill Nation," *New York Times*, June 18, 2011.

2. Frank R. Baumgartner, Jeffrey M. Berry, Marie Hojnacki, David C. Kimball, and Beth L. Leech, *Lobbying and Policy Change: Who Wins, Who Loses, and Why* (Chicago: University of Chicago Press, 2009), 6.

3. Paul Krugman, "A Tale of Two Moralities," *New York Times*, January 13, 2011. For systematic statements of this general view, see James Davison Hunter, *Culture Wars: The Struggle to Define America*

(New York: Basic Books, 1992); Stanley Greenberg, *The Two Americas: Our Current Political Deadlock and How to Break It* (New York: St. Martin's Press, 2005); and John Kenneth White, *Values Divide: American Politics and Culture in Transition* (Washington, DC: Congressional Quarterly Press, 2002).

4. Jonathan Rauch, "Bipolar Disorder," *Atlantic Monthly*, January/February 2005, 102–10. Rauch adds: "I'm joking. But the joke has a kernel of truth" (102). For a sample of the range of views on this theme, see Pietro S. Nivola and David W. Brady, eds., *Red and Blue Nation?*, vol. 1 (Washington, DC: Brookings Institution Press, 2006); and vol. 2 (Washington, DC: Brookings Institution Press, 2008). Also see the works cited at page 222, note 20 in the Introduction of the present volume.

5. Morris P. Fiorina, with Samuel J. Abrams and Jeremy C. Pope, *Culture War? The Myth of a Polarized America*, 3rd ed. (New York: Longman, 2010); Paul DiMaggio, John Evans, and Bethany Bryson, "Have Americans' Social Attitudes Become More Polarized?," *American Journal of Sociology* 19, no. 4 (1996): 690–755; and Alan Wolfe, *One Nation, After All: What Americans Really Think about God, Country, Family, Racism, Welfare, Immigration, Homosexuality, Work, The Right, The Left and Each Other* (New York: Penguin, 1999).

6. See David Mayhew's "Lists of Important Enactments of Congress" (updated through 2008), http://pantheon.yale.edu/~dmayhew/data3.html.

Acknowledgments

This book originated in our discussions and writings, beginning in 2007, about the difficulty of political compromise in democracy, a problem we thought deserved more attention than it had received. As we observed the changing scene in American politics, we came to believe that the general problem could be best addressed by concentrating on a particular institution, the United States Congress.

The first result of our work was an article, "Mindsets of Political Compromise," published in *Perspectives on Politics* (December 2010). The editor, Jeffrey Isaac, provided excellent advice on the manuscript. Many readers across a wide political spectrum offered us thoughtful observations on the issues raised in the article. Encouraged by their reactions, we set out to explore political compromise in the greater depth that a book would allow. We were fortunate that Princeton University Press saw the need to publish a book on this subject in a timely manner. We could not have had a more encouraging and discerning editor than Rob Tempio.

Sigal Ben-Porath, Russell Muirhead, Norman Ornstein, and Gregory Rost gave us invaluable comments on the entire manuscript. Erica Jaffe Redner, Leah Popowich, Adam Michaels, and Stephen Steinberg provided important assistance on particular parts. Michael Delli Carpini contributed helpful suggestions on the media, as did Diana Hess, on civic education. We also gratefully acknowledge financial support from the Spencer Foundation. We continue to be indebted to our students and colleagues who helped us develop our ideas over the years.

Index

Baumgartner, Frank R., 252n1
Beam, David R., 220n6
Beatles, The, 203
Beat the Press (WGBH), 197–98
Becerra, Xavier, 233n41
Bellantoni, Christina, 238n48
Benditt, Theodore M., 231n18
Benjamin, Martin, 231n20
Berry, Jeffrey M., 252n1
Besson, Samantha, 232n28
bias: Citizens Against ProObama
    Media Bias and, 250n75; cogni-
    tive, 67–68; media and, 196,
    250n75; mindsets and, 67
Biden, Joe, 136, 140, 238n50,
    239nn52,55
Binder, Sarah A., 243n7, 244nn10,
    12, 14
Bingaman, Jeff, 95
bipartisanship, 7, 230n12; econo-
    mizing on disagreement and,
    126–27, 133–40; mutual respect
    and, 114; 111th Congress and,
    133–40; Ornstein proposal and,
    169–70; Udall proposal and,
    168–69; unemployment benefits
    and, 134, 137. *See also* Compro-
    mise, bipartisan
Birnbaum, Jeffrey, 220n6, 227n40,
    228n41, 233n39, 235n14
Bishop, Bill, 222n21, 251n89
Blank, Rebecca, 226n26
Blasi, Vincent, 246n36
Blumenthal, Sidney, 219n1
Blumler, Jay G., 243n37
Boehner, John, 246n33; abortion
    and, 232n37; *Face the Nation*
    and, 135, 238n49; health care
    and, 86; media and, 63–64, 135,
    197, 238n49; principled pru-
    dence and, 102; *60 Minutes* and,
    63–64, 229n1
Bohman, James, 235n10
Bohner, Gerd, 229n3
Borah, Porismita, 229n4
Bowles, Erskine, 14, 221n15

Bowles-Simpson Commission, 142
Bradley, Bill, 6, 116, 146, 236n15
Brady, David, 225n17, 243n36,
    253n4
Brettschneider, Corey, 225n19
Brown, Carrie Budoff, 233nn48, 49,
    234nn52, 53
Brown, Scott, 44
Brownstein, Ronald, 222n20,
    236nn21–24, 237nn29, 35–36
Bryson, Bethany, 253n5
Buchanan, Pat, 88
Budget Control Act of 2011 (Debt
    Ceiling Act), 2, 9, 27, 140, 223n7
Burke, Edmund, 28, 70–71,
    224nn11, 12, 231nn13, 14, 15
Bush, George H. W., 87–88, 233n38
Bush, George W., 26, 236n18; Alito
    and, 173; Gang of Twelve and,
    93; immigration and, 93–94;
    Kerry and, 147, 240n4; Office of
    Political Affairs (OPA) and, 175;
    Pelosi and, 127; Rove and, 148,
    176; Social Security reform and,
    121; tax cuts of, 64, 134, 138

Cain, Bruce E., 245n24, 247n45,
    248nn46, 47
California, 61, 184–85
Calmes, Jackie, 238n50, 239nn52,
    53, 55
campaign finance, 155, 215;
    bundled contributions and, 182;
    contribution limits and, 183–84;
    democratic values and, 183–84;
    fundraising and, 66, 161–62,
    177, 180–84, 190, 205; Justice
    Stevens and, 181; political action
    committees (PACs) and, 183;
    time-protection argument and,
    180–84
campaigning: adversarial approach
    and, 150–51; Americanization
    of, 165; animosity hangover
    from, 151–52; attack ads and,
    150–51, 241n14; bargaining and,

confusion in, 36–37, 40–41,
53, 62, 207; considerations for
judging, 74–75, 101, 107–8;
costs of not compromising and,
30–35; decent vs. rotten, 78–79,
231nn21, 23; difficulty of, 1–2
(*see also* seeking compromise);
distinctive character of, 11, 36,
53–54, 80, 108, 231n18; distinguished from consensus, 12–13;
doubts about, 210–14; favorable
conditions for, 58–60, 77, 117,
228n51, 252n95; general value
of, 29–31, 62, 72, 101, 104, 209,
225n16; immediate threats and,
26–27; international, 11; legislative, 8, 11–12 (*see also* legislative compromise); limits of, 24,
26–27, 41–54; loopholes and,
6, 40, 50, 80–81; mindsets and,
16–24 (*see also* mindsets); moralized compromise procedure and,
110; mutual sacrifice and, 10,
17, 100, 150, 209; necessity of in
democracy, 27, 204; objections
to promoting, 2, 210–14 (*see also*
resisting compromise); path–
dependent attitudes and, 36–37;
process of, 2–5, 10, 17, 21–24,
27, 58–61 (*see also* democratic
process); public ambivalence
over, 25–26; spirit of, 1, 3, 24, 60,
98, 204; as surrender, 36, 39, 53;
valuing, 25–62(*see also* valuing
compromise); vulnerabilities of,
35–41, 53–54
Compromise of 1819–20, 55
Compromise of 1850, 55, 130
Compromise of 1877, 58
compromising mindset: campaigning and, 146, 148, 159–63,
171, 175, 183, 186, 199, 203–4;
characteristics of, 3–4, 16, 18–24;
conservatives and, 65; dilemma
of reform and, 214–17; doubts
and, 213–14; economizing on

disagreement and, 117–33; in
governing, 171, 175, 183, 186,
199, 203–4; legislature and, 175;
liberals and, 65; media and, 186,
199; principled prudence and,
100–106; resisting compromise
and, 65–66, 68, 88, 231n20; seeking compromise and, 100–101,
103, 105–6, 109–13, 117–18, 126,
128, 131–32, 139, 143; Udall
proposal and, 168; uses of, 208;
valuing compromise and, 40, 62.
See also mutual respect
conflict of values, 12
confusion, 36–37, 40–41, 53, 62, 207
Congress: campaigning and, 156,
162, 168–76, 182–83, 197,
242n27, 244n14, 245n25,
247n41; cloture rule and, 134,
173, 244n13; conflict with
president and, 20; divided, 1;
divided America and, 211–13;
do-nothing, 211–12; doubts about
compromise and, 211–12; duck-
ing responsibility and, 140–41;
economizing on disagreement
and, 117–40, 133, 139; mindsets
and, 20; 111th, 133–40; polarization and, 102 (*see also* polarization); redistricting and, 242n27,
247n45; reform and, 7 (*see also*
reform); resisting compromise
and, 63, 81, 83, 86–87, 90–93, 98;
seeking compromise and, 102–4,
119, 128, 131, 133, 136, 140–42;
sovereign debt limit and, 1; status
quo and, 2; sustained interaction
and, 168–70; Tax Reform Act
and, 5; term limits and, 177–79,
245nn24, 25; valuing compromise and, 25–26, 31, 38, 42–47,
54, 60, 223n7. *See also* legislative
compromise; Senate; House of
Representatives
Congressional Budget Office, 90
Conlan, Timothy J., 220n6

independents, 149, 160, 223n6
Indians, 57
integrative agreements, 14–16, 150
integrity: compromise as preserving,
231n20; law and, 81–83, personal, 164. *See also* principled
prudence
interests vs. principles, 73–78
intransigence, 43, 45, 91, 98, 122,
129, 167. *See also* uncompromising mindset
Iyengar, Shanto, 230n11, 240n11,
249nn64, 66, 67, 251nn84, 85

Jacobson, Gary C., 240n7
Jamieson, Kathleen Hall, 232n34,
240n11, 241n14, 249nn64–66,
68, 69
Jefferson, Thomas, 176–77
Jindal, Bobby, 239n57
Johnson, Lyndon B., 235n5; Civil
Rights Act and, 105; as consensus
man, 104–5; principled prudence
and, 104–5
Johnston, Richard, 240nn11, 12
Joint Select Committee on Deficit
Reduction, 141
Jones, Charles O., 219nn1, 3
Jones, Walter, Jr., 247n41
judicial nominations, 173
Just, Marion R., 250n78
justice: disagreement about, 39; in-
tegrity and, 81; immigration and,
93; as goal of governing, 159;
principles of, 74, 76, 77; opportu-
nities for, 101; social, 53; theory
of, 37, 108. *See also* fairness
Justice Department, 172

Kahne, Joseph, 252n94
Kahneman, Daniel, 230n11
Kamm, Frances, 226n21, 235nn8, 9
Kegan, Paul, 227n28
Kelly, Andrew P., 251n87
Kennedy, Ted, 19, 97, 104, 120,
236n20

Kentucky, 130, 131
Keren, Gideon, 229n2
Kernell, Samuel, 219n1
Kerry, John, 146–47, 239n3, 240n4
kickbacks, 48–49
Kimball, David C., 252n1
King, Anthony, 219n1, 245nn28, 29
King, Gary, 240n11
Kramer, Justin, 246n36
Krause, Sharon, 237n30
Krauthammer, Charles, 239n57
Krugman, Paul, 252n3
Kudlow, Larry, 238n49
Kuflik, Arthur, 220n11, 222n23
Kurland, Philip B., 231n13
Kurtz, Karl T., 245n24
Kuttner, Robert, 226n27
Kyl, Jon, 94

Larson, John, 247n41
Lau, Richard R., 241n13
Lautzenheiser, Daniel K., 251n87
leadership, 43–44, 183. *See also*
governing
Leech, Beth L., 252n1
legislative compromise, 8, 21, 23,
226n26; acceptable vs. unacceptable, 78–85; campaigning and,
146, 149, 164, 167, 170–73, 197;
character of, 10–16; classic, 12,
14, 16, 39, 41, 93, 131, 138, 193,
207, 212–13; cloture rule and,
134, 173, 244n13; Comprehensive Immigration Act of 2007
and, 92–97; consensual, 12 (*see
also* consensus); defusing the
agenda and, 121–23; dilemma
of reform and, 215; economizing
on disagreement and, 117–40;
loopholes and, 6, 40, 50, 80–81;
material interests and, 11; moral
perspectives and, 39; mutual
mistrust and, 85–99; poison pills
and, 121–22; principled prudence and, 100–109; principle
interests and, 11;

legislative compromise (*cont'd*)
resisting compromise and, 80–
82; restraining the rhetoric and,
123–25; seeking compromise
and, 104, 109–12, 142; separating
the issues and, 118–21; sustained
interaction and, 168–70; threat
of force and, 11; uncompromising mindset and, 85–99 (*see also*
uncompromising mindset); use
of mindsets and, 207–10; valuing
compromise and, 31, 36, 39–41,
44–46, 49–50
legislature: California, 61; collective achievements and, 169;
compromising mindset and, 175;
control shifts in, 122; distinctive
character of compromise in, 11;
fundraising and, 66, 161–62, 177,
180–84, 190, 205; individual
interactions and, 169; integrative
agreements and, 15; long-term
relationships and, 209; Madison
and, 188; media and, 192–93;
Michigan, 178; minority and, 7,
26, 102, 122, 129, 164–65, 172–
75; National Conference of State
Legislatures and, 252n95; reform
and, 183 (*see also* reform); state,
61, 178–79, 183, 252n95; status
quo and, 9; term limits and,
177–79, 245nn24, 25; uncompromising mindset and, 151; voting
foreknowledge and, 71. *See also*
Congress
Leonhardt, David, 239n56
Lepora, Chiara, 228n51
Lerner, Ralph, 231n13
Liberal Party, 74
liberals: as against compromise, 28;
change and, 32; compromising
mindset and, 65; environmental
issues and, 38; farm subsidies
and, 38; illegal immigrants and,
93; loopholes for wealthy and,
40; radicals and, 42, 226n27;

resisting compromise and, 32,
65, 93; uncompromising mindset
and, 65; valuing compromise
and, 28–29, 32, 38, 40, 42
liberty: principle of, 77, 158; slavery
and, 54; value of, 181. *See also*
free choice; freedom of the press;
free market; free speech
Lienesch, Michael, 229n56
Lizza, Ryan, 235nn12, 13
lobbyists, 161, 178, 211
logrolling, 15, 48
loopholes, 6, 40, 50, 80–81
Luban, David, 226n21
Luscombe, Belinda, 99–100, 234n1

McAvoy, Paula, 252n93
McCain, John, 97
McCarty, Nolan, 222n20, 247n45
McChesney, Robert, 251n83
McClurg, Scott D., 240n10
McConnell, Mitch, 136, 140, 165,
238n49
McConnell-Biden negotiations, 136,
140
McGrail, M. A., 237n30
McKersie, Robert, 221n16
Mackie, Gerry, 241n18
Madison, James, 33, 179, 188,
225n18, 228n54, 245nn30, 31,
249n63
Madonna, Anthony J., 244n10
majoritarianism, 8–9, 14, 223n7,
244n13; campaigning and, 148,
156, 172–74, 187; citizen support
and, 217; doubts about compromise and, 211; economizing on
disagreement and, 125, 128; principled prudence and, 102; principled tenacity and, 81; supermajority and, 102, 156, 172, 174, 217,
244n14; uncompromising mindset
and, 94, 141–42; valuing compromise and, 25–27, 45, 50
Mann, Thomas E., 219nn1, 2;
campaigning and, 242nn29, 31,

243nn4,6, 246n38, 247n42–45,
249n62; valuing compromise
and, 225n17
Mansbridge, Jane, 232n32
Marcuse, Herbert, 231n16
Margalit, Avishai, 78–79, 231nn21,
22, 23
Marriage Vow, 163
Martin, Philip L., 237n42
Massachusetts, 102
May, Simon Căbulea, 225n16
Mayer, Jacob Peter, 244n17
Mayhew, David, 219n1, 253n6
Mazzoli, Romano L., 131, 237n41
media: assumptions of, 191–92;
audience shares and, 190, bias
and, 196, 250n75; campaigning
and, 160–61, 168, 174, 182, 185–
99; candidates and, 190, 196–97;
career enhancement and, 133;
Citizens Against ProObama Media Bias and, 250n75; common
ground and, 193; compromising
mindset and, 186, 199; constructive political action and, 113;
distorting influence of, 2, 189–93;
economizing on disagreement
and, 122–23; Explanatory Reporting on Governing and, 198;
FactCheck.org and, 195, 250n75;
filibuster pivot and, 174; flip-
flopping and, 191; focus groups
and, 196; framing and, 66–67,
189–92, 199; freedom of the press
and, 196; fundamental change in,
249n64; governing and, 189–99;
horse race coverage and, 189,
196, 249nn64, 67; increased pressures from, 205; journalist interpretations and, 190–91, 195–97;
legislature and, 192–93; minding
of, 189–99; National Endowment
for Journalism and, 198; online,
193–95, 199, 251n85; pack journalism and, 197; permanent campaigns and, 24, 160; promotion

of understanding by, 197–98;
Pulitzer Prizes and, 198; reform
and, 188–89; reinforcement of
cynicism by, 85, 232n34; television and, 86, 191–94, 250n72;
uncompromising mindset and,
189–90, 195
Medicaid, 48, 139
Medicare, 139, 141
Mencken, H. L., 61, 229n57
Menendez, Robert, 239n57
Menkel-Meadow, Carrie, 221n18
Mexico, 93
Michel, Bob, 122
Michigan, 178
Mill, John Stuart, 28, 49, 107,
227n28, 235n7
Miller, Cheryl, 251n87
mindsets: bargaining and, 208; campaigning and, 65–66, 204; citizen
support and, 216–18; cognitive
bias and, 67–68; cognitive state
and, 65; common ground and,
207; competitive democracy
and, 206; of compromise, 10,
16–24; concept of, 64; context
and, 65; cynicism and, 61, 85–91,
95–96, 100, 109–17, 151, 190–
91, 232n34, 236n16, 242n31,
249n69; defined, 64–65; democracy and, 12, 23–24, 205–6, 214;
democratic process and, 3, 68,
206, 209, 224n10; dilemma of reform and, 214–16; dispositional
state and, 65; disrespect and, 66;
economizing on disagreement
and, 129–33; framing and, 66–
69; governing and, 204–5, 209;
individual judgment and, 29;
interests vs. principles and, 73–
78; lack of theory for, 69; makeup
of, 64–69; mixing of, 129–33,
205; morality and, 67, 69; mutual
mistrust and, 85–91, 90; mutual
respect and, 206–9; negotiation
and, 66; polarization and, 14,

mindsets (cont'd)
19, 21, 39, 102, 120, 126, 133,
139, 169, 174, 198, 205, 212–13;
political opposition and, 209;
principled prudence and, 16,
100–106, 109, 112, 120, 126, 129,
208; principled tenacity and, 69,
71, 85; resisting compromise and,
206; spirit of laws and, 204–5;
Tax Reform Act of 1986 and,
17–18, 21, 23; uses of, 205–10;
valuing compromise and, 29–30,
42, 62. See also compromising mindset; uncompromising
mindset
minorities, 7, 26, 102, 122, 129,
164–65, 172–75
moderates, 32, 42, 86, 91, 187,
236n25
Mondale, Walter, 5
Montgomery, Lori, 238n49
Moore, Barrington, Jr., 231n16
moralized compromise procedure,
110
morality: campaigning and, 21,
149–50, 200; cognitive bias and,
67–68; common ground and, 38;
Constitutional Convention and,
54; costs of not compromising
and, 35; differing views on, 38;
doubts about compromise and,
212; historical examples of, 54,
57–58; integrity and, 231n20;
kickbacks and, 48–49; legislative
compromise and, 39; limits of
compromise and, 41, 52; makeup
of mindsets and, 67, 69; Marriage
Vow and, 163; material interests
and, 76–78; middlemen and, 28;
mutual respect and, 110, 114,
117; partisanship and, 133; prag-
matism and, 225n16; principled
prudence and, 101, 106–9; principled tenacity and, 73–83; pro
tanto wrongs and, 228n51; tax reform and, 6–7; uncompromising

mindset and, 93; violations of,
75; weighing factors and, 226n21.
See also ethics
Moran, Simone, 229n2
Morley, John, 224n10
motive cynicism, 236n16; mutual
mistrust and, 85–90; mutual
respect and, 109–17; uncompromising mindset and, 96
Mouffe, Chantal, 227n28
Moynihan, Daniel Patrick, 146
Muirhead, Russell, 237nn30, 31
Murkowski, Lisa, 236n26
Murray, Alan, 220n6, 227n40,
228n41, 233n39, 235n14
Murray, Shailagh, 234n3, 238n49
mutual mistrust: adjustment of will
and, 90; adversarial approach
and, 150–51; Boehner and, 64;
Buchanan and, 88; campaigning
and, 150, 204; campaign promises and, 87–88; Clinton and, 88;
Comprehensive Immigration Act
of 2007 and, 92–97; cynicism
and, 61, 85–91, 95–96, 100,
109–17, 151, 190–91, 232n34,
236n16, 242n31, 249n69; death
panels and, 123–24; defined, 17;
Democrats and, 86–91; economizing on disagreement and,
120, 122; fear and, 33; George H.
W. Bush and, 87–88; health-
care debate and, 86, 90–91;
House of Representatives and,
86, 89; inflammatory rhetoric
and, 123–24; mindsets and,
85–91; multiplication of, 91–99;
negotiation and, 89; O'Neill and,
89–90; political opposition and,
86–87; Republicans and, 86, 89;
resisting compromise and, 85–
91; respect and, 109; role of, 208;
Tax Reform Act and, 91; uncompromising mindset and, 85–99,
109, 150; willful opposition and,
64, 85–86